AROUND LONDON BY TROLLEYBUS

PART ONE

By Hugh Taylor

TITLE PAGE

Finchley depot only played a minor role in service provision for route 660 so most photographs of trolleybuses on this route are Stonebridge vehicles. J1 928 belongs to Finchley and is at the north end of Chichele Road at Cricklewood Broadway on 13th March 1955. Note the feeder pillar on the right hand pavement; guard wires are attached to the adjoining traction pole and deflect dewired trolley arms – their role prevents damage to windows of nearby buildings. (Peter Mitchell 6819)

D2 404 is in Bexley Road, Northumberland Heath working on route 698 on 21st February 1959. This vehicle was allocated to Hanwell depot when new but soon moved on to Hammersmith. It had arrived at Bexleyheath by December 1940 where it suffered a small amount of wartime damage with the repair costing a mere £3. It was very badly damaged when the depot was hit by an enemy bomb on 29th June 1944. It was repaired 'in-house' and spent the rest of its days working on routes 696 and 698. (Peter Mitchell 12188)

ISBN 978-1-874422-98-3
Publication no. 102
Published in 2014 by Adam Gordon, Kintradwell Farm, Brora, Sutherland KW9 6LU.
Tel: 01408 622660
E-mail: adam@ahg-books.com

Designed, Typeset & Printed by Henry Ling Limited, at the Dorset Press, Dorchester DT1 1HD

AUTHOR'S NOTE

Over the years I have amassed thousands of photographs of London trolleybuses, but estimate that only four percent are worthy of publication; of those, only a small number are worth enlarging. I have been putting them aside on the basis that one day I would use them in a 'la crème de la crème' book about these vehicles. I have always been grateful to those who allowed me access to their material but did not want to publish without using Peter Mitchell's pictures. I had seen them on two occasions and they were the best of all; these have now become available to me. Therefore the time has come to publish 'Around London by Trolleybus'. Most photographs have never been seen before – none of Peter Mitchell's or John Clarke's. This part deals with South, West and North-West London. Many people are interested in destination blinds and throughout the book readers are encouraged to look at the different displays used by various depots to describe the same location. The reader will notice that a number of the black and white photographs are in full page landscape layout; some of Peter Mitchell's photographs were so good that it was thought best to present them in this way so that the reader could view them to full advantage. The opportunity has also been taken to illustrate the colour images in this way.

It turns out that and Peter and John were friends in the past, so it is appropriate that the sterling efforts that they made to record the passing London trolleybus scene are illustrated together. Adam Gordon has been an excellent proof reader and Roger Smith has produced the map. Iain Robinson of Henry Ling Ltd has done an excellent job with the layout. Last but definitely not the least is 'my little piranha fish' – my wife Catherine – who has gone far beyond the call of duty in the final preparations and helped very much with her word processing skills.

I had a niche at Isleworth depot between 6th January and 8th May 1962. During that time London Transport held a last trolleybus driving school embracing three of their conductors; I found it intriguing that it started so late in the trolleybus era and two of them and myself struck up a friendship, which as a young lad I appreciated. The Daily Mail, in their 'Missing and found' column located Adrian O'Callaghan (T14898) who told me, forty-seven years later, why this driving school was activated in February 1962. Terry Shaw (T14876) saw the article and having lost contact with him in about 1990, got in touch with me. Both are pictured in this book and I dedicate it to them.

If anybody wants to communicate with me they can do so on: isleworthdepot@trolleybus.net

Hugh Taylor, Edgware, Middlesex

The clouds darken as N1 1590 leaves Bromyard Avenue in Acton Vale in the evening of 27th May 1960. There were no scheduled short-workings to this point on the 666 so 1590 has been running late and has been curtailed. The destination blind display for Edgware is for route 664, however, the via points are still relevant but it would have been more appropriate to use the 666 display, as it showed Acton and Cricklewood as via points. Bromyard Avenue loop was extensively used – 607s and 655s were scheduled to turn there as were a few 660s. (Peter Mitchell 14660)

CONTENTS

SOUTH LONDON

DARTFORD TO ABBEY WOOD VIA BEXLEYHEATH

Trolleybuses did not play a major part in the transport needs of South London. Tram routes still operating in this area at the end of the Second World War were not converted to trolleybus operation; motorbuses took the place of their rail-bound counterparts.

Stages two and three of a programme that would see more than half of London's trams replaced by trolleybuses between 1935 and 1940 featured routescentring on Bexleyheath; the main reason for nominating these routes for early conversion was the dilapidated state of the track in the area. On 10th November 1935 route 698 was inaugurated, operating between Bexleyheath Market Place and Woolwich Ferry via Erith. Due to the track layout at Abbey Wood, passengers had to change there; with the introduction of trolleybuses they could now make their journeys uninterrupted. Exactly two weeks later, on 24th November, route 696 commenced; working between Dartford Market Street and Woolwich Ferry via Crayford, Bexleyheath, Welling it was a busy route with no real help until the 698 joined it at Plumstead Corner. Both ran from a brand new depot in Erith Road, Bexleyheath as both Erith and Bexleyheath tram depots could not be adapted for trolleybuses. When ordering vehicles for this area,

London Transport considered that sixty-seaters would be sufficient to cope with the volume of passengers expected. Within weeks, the demand was so high that any spare and new vehicles were pressed into service until some seventy-seaters arrived; the phenomenal increase in loadings could not have been anticipated. There were a number of reasons for this: 1) Housing development 2) Increased work at Woolwich Arsenal, 3) A much better mode of transport. Passenger loadings continued to rise, particularly in the Woolwich area; Britain was gearing up its armament programme in anticipation of war with Germany. The increased requirement was met by sending in more seventy-seaters; this was still not enough so in the summer of 1939 most of the sixty-seaters were replaced by those with a carrying capacity of seventy.

Those wishing to travel between Bexleyheath and Woolwich would use the 696 as it was far quicker than the 698 which meandered through Barnehurst, Erith and Abbey Wood. Dartford was the easternmost point of the trolleybus system and the only town served by trolleybuses but not Central buses.

There were few service alterations in this area. Between May 1937 and April 1944 a Sunday and Bank Holiday 694 worked between Woolwich Ferry and Erith via Welling and Bexleyheath; it had rather a fitful existence but when it did operate, gave a 'round the corner' facility at

Leaving Dartford Market Place on 5th October 1957, D2B 405B is working on route 696 to Woolwich. As opposed to Central Bus practice whereby conductor and driver each had a timecard, trolleybus staff had one between them; in this instance the driver has possession of it and has placed it in the front nearside windscreen. 405B had been rebodied by East Lancashire Coach Builders in the aftermath of the near destruction of Bexleyheath depot on 29th June 1944. On return to London it continually worked on routes 696 and 698. It was the last trolleybus into Bexleyheath depot, at 1.15am on Wednesday 4th March 1959, and closed stage one of the trolleybus conversion programme. (Peter Mitchell 10420)

807 picks up passengers in Dartford High Street; the bus stop flag has room for nine E plate numbers – only one is used and that is for route 696. H1 807 is only going as far as Welling Corner; there were many short-workings and odd journeys operated on the 'Bexley system' that catered for the needs of workers in the area. (R C Stevens)

In connection with London Transport's programme for substituting trolleybuses for trams on 148 miles of route, the tram routes set out below will be converted to trolleybus routes on the dates shown

Date	Tram Route		Trolleybus Route
Nov. 10	40	Section WOOLWICH (Beresford Square) and ABBEY WOOD	698	WOOLWICH (Free Ferry) Erith and BEXLEYHEATH Every 7 minutes
	98	ABBEY WOOD Erith and BEXLEYHEATH		
Nov. 24	96	WOOLWICH (Beresford Square) Welling and HORNS CROSS	696	WOOLWICH (Free Ferry) Welling and DARTFORD (Market Street) Every 4 minutes to Bexleyheath Every 7 minutes to Dartford

Note: The tram track between Dartford and Horns Cross will be abandoned. A cheap return fare for workmen will be available on the frequent service of motor buses operating over the section of the tramway to be abandoned.

Tram Routes 36 and 38 will continue to operate between Abbey Wood, Woolwich, and Victoria Embankment.

TIMES of first and last trolleybuses are shown overleaf.

Starting on March 4, 1959

BUSES FOR TROLLEYBUSES

Bexleyheath, Crayford, Dartford, Erith and Woolwich Area

TIMETABLES

SERVICE INTERVALS

TIMES OF FIRST AND LAST BUSES

LONDON TRANSPORT
55 Broadway, S.W.I ABBey 1234

Information leaflet about forthcoming trolleybus routes in the Bexleyheath area.

The driver and conductor happily pose for the photographer; whether he wanted a trolleybus that had Alhambrinal panelling in the lower deck or not will never be known but he has provided an excellent view of 107A, one of five trolleybuses rebodied by Weymann's in the early part of the war that had this feature. Note also the sliding windows that were fitted to these vehicles rather than half-drops. Bexleyheath depot changed from the punch and rack system to Gibson ticket machines on 18th July 1954 – this view therefore was taken prior to that date. (R C Stevens)

407B effortlessly climbs West Hill, Dartford on the first part of its journey to Woolwich on route 696. Vehicles rebodied by East Lancs, these and the C suffixed vehicles, could be distinguished from other members of the fleet by not having a ventilator above the nearside windscreen; this was a typical feature of their rebodying. The steepness of the hill is well-illustrated by 407B passing Dartford Hospital on 5th October 1957. (Peter Mitchell 10419)

An interesting feature on the 'Bexley network' was the reversing triangle at Princes Road, Crayford; six vehicles turned in Monday to Friday evenings, catering for workers at the nearby Vickers factory. 766B has just reversed – it displays CRAYFORD PRINCESS ROAD, a blind compiler's error as PRINCES ROAD was the correct spelling. 390B waits its turn. An inspector was stationed here to oversee the difficult movements. (Denis Battams)

D2 410 passes Crayford Town Hall while working to WOOLWICH FERRY on 1st May 1954. Three days earlier (on 28th April), London Transport had announced that the trolleybus system was to be abandoned. (Peter Mitchell 5519)

The Saturday afternoon frequency of route 698 was not sufficient enough to carry the many shoppers who wanted to travel as far as Erith; to accommodate the need extras were run between Bexleyheath Market Place and STATION ROAD ERITH. Performing one of these trips on 7th February 1959 is rebodied trolleybus D2C 98C; note the lack of a ventilator over the nearside windscreen, a feature of these vehicles. (Ron Wellings)

The Bexleyheath Coronation Memorial Clock Tower, commemorating the coronation of King George V, was formally opened on Bexleyheath Gala Day, 17 July 1912; H1 789, on route 696 to Dartford, moves past it on 23rd February 1959. The bronzed framed request stop is mounted on a stub post which is bracketed from a concrete post. 789 passes through the 698 crossover at the Market Place. (Peter Mitchell 12205)

Entering Bexleyheath depot is 395B. The conductor is conscientious as BEXLEYHEATH DEPOT is displayed; this is just a short run from Bexleyheath Market Place but it is possible that there might be a passenger or two who might want to make such a journey on route 698. Once 395B has moved off the highway, RT 4359 on route 122 can continue its trip to Woolwich. (Jack Gready)

Due to the lack of traffic, a first glance at this photograph gives the impression that it was taken on a Sunday; this is not so as it is Monday 17th June 1957. H1 798 is outside Bexleyheath depot on route 698. Note the single bowstring bracket arm on the depot forecourt; the white painted bases to the traction standards assist staff to know their position in the dark. (John Clarke)

D2s had to be brought onto the Bexleyheath routes very early on due to passenger growth in the area. 410 is in Belvedere on 23rd August 1958. The 698 was a quieter route in terms of passenger numbers than the 696 and a welcome relief from the busyness of that service for the crews. (Clarence Carter)

H1B 790B is allocated to route 698 on 21st February 1959 and is seen on Belvedere Railway bridge. Routes 696 and 698 were withdrawn after service on 3rd March 1959. Only eight of Bexleyheath's trolleybuses survived conversion stage one; 790B was not one of them and it was towed to a breaker's yard at Charlton on 8th April. (Peter Mitchell 12185)

Working on route 698, D2 423 picks up passengers in Abbey Wood. The trolleybus is not the main subject; the most prominent item is the overhead. Three crossovers feature conspicuously against the sky; electricity is fed into the overhead on both the westbound and eastbound tracks. A vestige of an earlier form of electric traction can be seen in the foreground – tram rails.

The photographer has captured six trolleybuses at Bexleyheath Market Place in one image – drivers have been able to get four vehicles onto the shunt wire. However, there were instances of a fourth vehicle not quite clearing the facing frog and the driver of a 696 from Dartford not noticing this – catastrophic results! The only identifiable trolleybus is H1 806 which is working to Woolwich on route 696 on 7th February 1959. (Ron Wellings)

About a third of the vehicles allocated to Bexleyheath depot were of the rebodied variety. Illustrating this feature, 786B is at Welling Corner on 23rd August 1958 working on route 696 to Woolwich. Pedestrian and vehicular traffic is heavy. (Clarence Carter)

Bexleyheath depot suffered two bomb attacks during World War Two; the second one (on 29th June 1944) saw a number of vehicles totally destroyed with many others needing new bodies – one that came into the latter category was D2 390. It was sent to East Lancs returning as D2B 390B. Route 696 has only eight days to go when this view was taken on 23rd February 1959 at Upper Wickham Lane by Okehampton Common. The driver could have made a better job of displaying DARTFORD MKT ST; however, this may be deliberate so that he does not have to change the blind at each end of the route. Going the other way, a 696 continues its journey to Woolwich. (Peter Mitchell 12206)

Rebodied 470B, on route 696, heads for Dartford; It is about to pass through the facing frog that leads to the short-working point in Villacourt Road. Beyond, in Wickham Lane, a bus stands outside Plumstead Bus Garage. (Don Thompson)

Heading east, routes 696 and 698 parted company at Plumstead Corner where 390B, a 696 to Dartford, is about to turn right into Wickham Lane; these two routes meet up again at Bexleyheath. The shop on the corner of Amrose Street has its three sun blinds fully opened. (John Clarke)

D2 416 is seen by Bannockburn school in Plumstead High Street on 21st February 1959 while working on route 696 to Woolwich. 476 languished in Bexleyheath depot for almost a month, before being towed away for scrap. (Peter Mitchell 12175)

The original terminus for trolleybuses at Woolwich was at Market Hill. By 1943, conditions were causing major problems – not only was there a tram conduit changeover pit to contend with, but bus route 75 also terminated there. All in all it had become too congested and cramped for three forms of transport. Consequently on 14th July that year, trolleybuses were extended to Parsons Hill. However the original loop, pictured here, was retained for emergency use. Two trams are receiving the attention of the plough pit attendant. H1 800 waits for the westbound tram's trolley arm to be taken off the positive trolleybus overhead; its rear blind has already been changed for the return trip to Bexleyheath on route 698.

On 29th September 1956, D2 476 turns into Parsons Hill where it will stand for a few minutes before returning to Bexleyheath on route 698. All traction poles on the extension from Woolwich Ferry to Parsons Hill had a C suffix added to its number – in view is C12. (Peter Mitchell 9357)

A sad vista compared to the previous view. Still showing the destination of its last journey on 3rd March 1959 D2 476 passes the now redundant overhead at Parsons Hill on 8th April 1959. George Cohen and company won the contract to break up the London trolleybuses in the 1959 to 1962 period. All those from Bexleyheath depot had to be towed. George Cohen was the biggest constituent in THE 600 GROUP of companies; one of their lorries tows 476 to the scrapyard at Penhall Road, Charlton. (Fred Ivey)

A number of trolleybuses withdrawn from Bexleyheath depot on the night of 3rd March 1959 stand forlornly in Penhall Road scrapyard awaiting their fate. Identifiable are 784B, 413, 471 and 439. In the immediate foreground are the remnants of tram rails – this had been the breaking-up yard for London trams between 1950 and 1953. (Fred Ivey)

Bexleyheath -these journeys previously operated without a route number. Due to an increasing number of vehicles using the terminus at Woolwich Ferry (bus route 75 as well as the trolleybuses) it became very cramped so on 14th July 1943 the route was extended to Woolwich, Parsons Hill; this was the last addition of wiring to the system (the only amendments thereafter were revisions or diversions).

From November 1935 until July 1952, trams and trolleybuses operated alongside each other between Abbey Wood and Woolwich. This was a very interesting aspect in London Transport's history and the longest period of dual operation between these two modes of transport in the capital. Until July 1952, the only means for people travelling by road transport to and from Abbey Wood was by tram or trolleybus.

Transport became Luftwaffe targets and on 7th November 1940 a bomb exploded on Bexleyheath depot with four vehicles needing new bodies. Far worse was a doodlebug hitting the premises with devastating consequences in the early hours of 29th June 1944; twelve vehicles were destroyed and twenty-six needed rebodying. No trolleybuses operated that morning. London Transport rose to the occasion and drafted vehicles in from all over the system, enabling a good service to be run that evening.

There were two unusual visitors to the area. First was Q1 1856 that had received a severe rear-end shunt while working on route 607 from Hanwell depot; it was sent to Charlton Works with the repair staff giving it a test drive on the 'Bexley system' before releasing it. 1856 was towed to and from Bexleyheath with the sortie occurring on 9th August 1956. Second, Q1 1779 crossed the River Thames by way of the Woolwich Ferry; this was a Fulwell training vehicle with the instructor wanting to privately see colleagues at Bexleyheath depot.

The routes in this area, which were the only London trolleybus services to operate in the county of Kent, had more complexities than in any other part of London; this was mainly for workers at Woolwich Arsenal and Vickers aircraft factory at Crayford. Some journeys from Woolwich to Dartford operated via the 698; particularly interesting were six evening journeys to various destinations from Crayford. Just three reversing triangles were used in London, two being in this area – at Crayford, Princes Road and Plumstead Station; trainee drivers were given extensive training on them with the one at Plumstead needing inch perfect positioning. The service level on route 698 was not adequate enough on Saturday afternoons to cater for shoppers, so extras ran between Bexleyheath and Erith to accommodate them.

In the post-war years, the trolleybuses operating from Bexleyheath were of great interest as about a third was of the re-bodied variety. Not only was there varying body styles, but there was different colour seating and décor. Because the Bexley services were an isolated outpost they were placed in pole position in the trolleybus conversion programme with stage one seeing routes 696 and 698 last operate on Tuesday 3rd March 1959. Despite the immense part that trolleybuses had played in the war, there was no public interest in the abandonment and the routes faded away without a whimper.

CRYSTAL PALACE TO SUTTON

Next on the conversion agenda were two tram routes that terminated in Croydon – one to Sutton, the other to Crystal Palace; the two were to be joined. The latter route used open-top cars which did not fit the LTPB's new image and had to go as soon as possible. It had been anticipated that the Sutton to West Croydon section would open on 13th October 1935 with that to Crystal Palace starting on 27th October; insufficient vehicles were available for either conversion to take place and was just one example of projected opening dates not being met. On 8th December 1935, route 654 commenced working between Sutton Green and West Croydon; on 9th February 1936 the Crystal Palace section was opened, enabling through running to start.

There were many twists and turns of the roadway on the 654 and sixty-seater B1 class vehicles were deemed appropriate; they had coasting and run-back brakes, these being a requirement for operation on Anerley Hill. At the bottom of the hill (at Thicket Road) the third reverser on the system was seen; this was principally for use when icy conditions made Anerley Hill inaccessible. Intriguingly, it had one scheduled journey there; this was at 2.52am on Coronation day 1953, providing an especially early facility for those wanting to get into Croydon for onward transit to town. Whether anyone travelled on this trip – or even knew about it – is open to question. When severe frosts occurred, trolleybuses ran all night to keep the wires clean; the vehicles used on these nocturnal outings had ice-cutting skids inserted in the trolley heads. On one occasion a member of the public needed to get to Croydon urgently in the middle of the night; he arrived at Crystal Palace, not anticipating that 654s would be running, but hoping that he might be able to obtain a lift from a passing motorist. Lo and behold though, there was a trolleybus with its saloon lights out and the volunteer driver having a few minutes rest. Explaining the situation, the driver allowed the man to travel with him.

The 654 worked from Sutton depot whose title was changed to Carshalton in July 1950; this route passed though Norwood, Selhurst, Croydon and Wallington which was the most southerly place reached by London trolleybuses. There was no other means of travelling between Croydon and Sutton than by trolleybus – to cope with this, a high frequency service was always provided on the 654. For a few days in September 1958, three seventy-seater J3s, normally seen on 'hilly route' 611, were used; they covered for some B1s that had been driven through floodwater and were out of action – having coasting and run-back brakes fitted they 'saved the day'. Another interesting feature of the 654 was the turning circle at Waddon Station which was not equipped with frogs or crossovers so a bamboo pole was required. There were a few scheduled trips from the Croydon direction but none from the other end; however, on busy Saturdays, extras were run from Crystal Palace to Waddon, meaning that the whole circle of wiring got a bit of polish. On 2nd June 1957, the highest numbered trolleybus on the fleet (1891) visited Carshalton depot on an enthusiast's tour.

Because it had the oldest vehicles in the fleet, route 654 was targeted for early withdrawal in the trolleybus conversion programme. The last day of operation was Tuesday 3rd March 1959 – with indecent haste, some vehicles were off to the scrapyard the next morning.

B1 67 is at Crystal Palace roundabout on 21st February 1959. There are just eleven days to go before stage one of the conversion programme starts; route 654 is one of three services that feature in this historic event in London Transport's annals. Pedestrians and motorists are probably unaware of the impending change – note the Daimler car on the right. (Peter Mitchell 12195)

Having circled Crystal Palace roundabout on 4th October 1956, B1 80 will soon come to a halt at the compulsory stop at the top of Anerley Hill. Having parked up, the driver will put his coasting brake lever into position and the conductor will place a scotch under a rear nearside wheel. The traction standard on the right supports heavy duty cables which are connected to the adjacent section box – they feed power to the running wires. (John Clarke)

An announcement by London Transport in 1946 stated that the South London trams would be replaced by motorbuses rather than trolleybuses which had been the original plan; this meant that the only trolleybus route to operate solely in South London was the 654. Seen at the junction of Northcote Road and Sydenham Road at Selhurst on 19th July 1958, B1 69 heads for Carshalton depot, its home since delivery in November 1935. (Peter Mitchell 11477)

There was a progressive switch of the manufacturing of trolleybus blinds from Charlton Works to Aldenham Works in 1951/1952; there was also an amalgamation of the Central Bus Department with the Tram and Trolleybus Department on 12th July 1950. The latter event saw the renaming of a number of trolleybus depots: for example, Sutton became Carshalton. The two departments do not seem to know what the other is doing as 74 shows SUTTON DEPOT on an Aldenham-manufactured blind. In June 1956, B1 74 on the 654 is on its way home as it passes through West Croydon; by now a CN code plate is fitted. (Tony Wright)

For nine days In September 1958, three J3s from Highgate depot were loaned to Carshalton; this was because a number of B1s were out of action, having been driven through heavy floodwater. The J3s and L1s were the only other vehicles in the fleet that were equipped with coasting and run-back brakes – their usual haunt was route 611 which required trolleybuses that had this equipment. J3 1050, working on route 654 to Crystal Palace, overtakes F1 656 which is on the 630 stand at West Croydon. (Fred Ivey)

B1 69 halts in Waddon to pick up two passengers on what is already a healthy load. Bus stop flags were often fitted to traction standards, but in this instance it has not happened. Route 654 was the preserve of the B1s. There are a number of bowstring bracket arms here; note the hexagonal street lamp. (Ronald Bristow)

490 was one of five B1s delivered in September 1936 and allocated to Holloway depot; it was quite a time before 489 – 493 came over to Sutton depot. 490 is at The Chase on Stafford Road (just south of Waddon Station) at 5.20pm on 14th May 1955. With a boosted frequency at this time of the day, it is not surprising that another 654 has caught it up. Due to its poor condition 490 was rejected upon entering the overhaul system in June 1957 – it was withdrawn and was the first of the second batch of B1s to succumb. (Peter Mitchell 7209)

B1s 66 and 76 are over the maintenance pits in Sutton depot. The stores area is on the left; presumably these were constructed after the overhead was installed as trolleybuses are unable to access these wires. The traverser incorporates a turntable which has been constructed by S. H. Heywood who installed them at a number of depots; it is capable of holding ten tons. Sutton was an early conversion from trams to trolleybuses and is typical of the high standard of construction; the rear of the depot is of characteristic layout with pits beyond the traverser. Much of the roof is made up of skylights which made it a good working area. (London Transport Museum U22373)

Carshalton's trolleybuses, that had been withdrawn on the night of 3rd March 1959, were moved out in the days following. On Monday 9th March, B1 93 leads two others out of the depot. They will travel via the erstwhile 654 route to Croydon, then the 630 wiring to Wandsworth, where they will follow route 628 to Craven Park. From there they will follow the 666 routeing to arrive at Colindale depot. Their poles will be dropped and they will move on battery power into the adjacent road. All will be parked up in the scrapyard. One Monday they are working for their living with London Transport – the next Monday they are in the breaker's yard. (John L Smith)

Seen at Sutton Green is 76 whose destination blind is set for Crystal Palace, the other end of route 654. B1 76 retains an off-side conductor's signalling window; this was an original feature that soon fell into disuse. The bus stop flag is unique and lists seven places served by 654s; the fluted traction pole stands in private land. Chef tomato ketchup is still available, but Croydon's Stockwell and Oxford furniture house has long gone. (Geoff Rixon)

CROYDON TO WANDSWORTH

Route 654 only had a tenuous link with the rest of the system; this was in Croydon where it linked up with the 630. The two routes ran alongside each other from West Croydon to Pitlake where, due to a very tight turn and to avoid vehicles meeting, a signal light system (operated by trolley heads touching an overhead skate) was installed. Route 630 worked between West Croydon and Harlesden (junction of Scrubs Lane with Harrow Road). For more than half of its life the northern terminus was described as NR WILLESDEN JUNCTION on destination blinds; it was not until the mid-1950s that it became known as HARLESDEN COLLEGE PARK (a public house, not a recreational facility). At inception it was, at 14.65 miles, London's longest trolleybus route. This distinction was lost to the 655 in July 1946 but the 630 remained London's longest daily trolleybus route. Intriguingly, the 630 and 655 worked over a common section – Wandsworth to Hammersmith. Both services had seventy-seven minutes end to end running time.

The 630 was an extremely busy service passing through Mitcham, Tooting, Wandsworth, Putney, Hammersmith and Shepherds Bush. It is difficult to achieve regular headways on long routes and, coupled with increasing traffic congestion, bunching of 630s was frequent especially in Monday to Friday evening peak hours. However, an abundance of short-working facilities enabled inspectors to regulate the route reasonably well at these times. The 630 was one of four routes that crossed the River Thames at Putney Bridge. Between Croydon and Mitcham the 630 was on its own and a fast run was usually guaranteed across Mitcham Common; at Wandsworth it joined those from Clapham Junction.

The southern end of route 630 hosted two very interesting aspects. It was practice on Christmas Day for all trolleybuses to be in their depots by 4pm; Hammersmith depot was a long way from West Croydon and therefore could not provide late afternoon journeys beyond Mitcham Fair Green. To cover this, Sutton depot worked between West Croydon and Figges Marsh, Mitcham where trolleybuses reversed on their batteries. Although it was only necessary for three journeys to connect with the last three 630s turning at Mitcham, nine trips were made; it would have raised eyebrows if the three journeys had each been a complete duty. It did at least give the Sutton crews a break from the daily Sutton to Crystal Palace routine. Sutton also worked the Mitcham section, providing extras on Mitcham Fair days and were even seen as far north as Summerstown on Coronation Day 1953. The second aspect concerned SUMMERSTOWN where greyhound racing was held at Wimbledon stadium. Overhead was erected along Wimbledon Road to enable 'dog specials' to operate from BROADWAY TOOTING on Monday, Wednesday and Friday evenings; until January 1940, trams had operated these journeys, working over some otherwise disused tracks. This turn-back was also used as a curtailment point from the other direction on route 630.

The 612 operated between Mitcham, Fair Green and Battersea, Princes Head. It had no individual features or items of interest and used the same wires as the 630 between Mitcham and Wandsworth; in fact the only area where it 'ran solo' was on the uninspiring section between Wandsworth and Battersea – even then there were parallel tram services. When each section of route was due to be opened, an inspection by the Ministry of Transport and Civil Aviation took place. In the case of the 612, this occurred on 8th September 1937; the service started on 12th September (the short gap between the two events was commonplace). In April 1944, Wandsworth depot was given a small weekday allocation on the 630; by this time they were working on route 628 on Bank Holidays. Although Wandsworth depot still operated trams, staff normally worked on just one mode of transport. The 612 featured in the first stage of the South London tram replacement programme; the reason for its withdrawal on 30th September 1950 was that Wandsworth changed from electrically powered vehicles to diesel buses in one go. This was the first instance of route mileage loss.

Route 628 worked between Clapham Junction and Harlesden Craven Park; for a fifteen month period (August 1938 to November 1939) it was extended to Wembley for greyhound and speedway racing at the nearby stadium. Routes 612 and 628 had a night service since inception; this operated until September 1950 after which a 630 night route ran; the 628/630 'nighters' did not run further north than Hammersmith. The 626 was a weekday peak hour service, operating between Clapham Junction and Acton Market Place; few would travel the length of the 626 as it was quicker to change onto a 660/666 at Hammersmith. From January 1951, Stonebridge was given an allocation on the 628 along with a few journeys on the 626; this was discontinued in January 1959. On Bank Holidays thereafter though, Stonebridge were recalled to the 628 giving their staff the luxury of travelling through Fulham, Putney, Wandsworth and on to Clapham Junction again! From 7th January 1959, the overhead between Wandsworth and Clapham Junction was only served in peak hours by the 626 and extension of route 655; the 628, which continued to operate daily, had been withdrawn at these times the previous day.

Extras were provided for the Boat Race which was always well patronised by spectators during the trolleybus era. On the last occasion that they were scheduled for this event (Saturday 2nd April 1960), it was hoped that the following would suffice for the Boat Race and other sporting events in the area. Although it could not be guaranteed that all would run, a priority was given for the 'break' after the race. EXTRAs depended on crews working additional hours and were normally operated by depots allocated to the routes; in the case of the 628 though, Stonebridge participated as their staff were cognisant with it.

628	4 vehicles	1–8pm	Shepherds Bush – Clapham Junction
630	4 vehicles	1–8pm	Harrow Road – Edgarley Terrace
655	3 vehicles	12–8pm	Hanwell – Hammersmith
657	3 vehicles	12–8pm	Hounslow – Shepherds Bush
667	6 vehicles	12–8pm	Hampton Court – Hammersmith

K2 1202 is just starting a journey on London Transport's longest daily trolleybus route – the 630 which works between West Croydon and Harlesden; behind is another K2 – 1327. RT 3148 is also on West Croydon stand with its next trip being to Godstone Garage on route 409; maybe they have a shortage of intermediate blinds as a side blind is used at the front. It is 2nd July 1960 so route 630 has just less than three weeks to go. (Peter Mitchell 15355)

In the post-war period there was only one place where trams crossed trolleybuses at right angles on the overhead system. This was at Croydon where 1701, working on route 630 to NR WILLESDEN JUNCTION, pauses at the traffic lights in Station Road at its junction with London Road. Passing southbound on tram route 16 is an unidentified Feltham working to CROYDON PURLEY.

1706 is north-west of Factory Lane (which is off Mitcham Road) on 25th February 1956 – this is not far from Pitlake. Traction poles could only be fitted on one side of the road so bowstring bracket arms sufficed on this stretch of route 630. P1 1706 was a long term resident of Hammersmith depot; its final nine months were spent at Edmonton. (Peter Mitchell 8461)

1279 is in Purley Way on 20th June 1960 heading for West Croydon on the 630; it passes a typical 1960s shopping parade with its various styles of sun blinds. 1279 will only be in service for another month; it was held in store until October when it was sold for scrap. (Peter Mitchell 15284)

On 18th April 1960, K1 1279 is at Mitcham Fair Green working to the northern terminus of route 630. With 'last full overhaul' dates dictating the length of time trolleybuses remained operational during the conversion period, 1279 did not fare very well. Receiving its last overhaul in August 1954 meant a shorter life rather than a longer one. It was transferred from Walthamstow to Hammersmith at stage two with the aim of withdrawing it at stage seven – the plan worked and 1279 along with many other Ks at Hammersmith depot were retired at this time. (Peter Mitchell 14375)

1076, on its way to Harlesden on the 630 on 2nd July 1960, is halfway across Mitcham Common – to be precise it is at the junction of Windmill Road with Beddington Lane. Drivers would have their charges on top notch across the Common. 1076 spent its last year at Hammersmith depot; previously it had been at Edmonton and Walthamstow. (Peter Mitchell 15350)

1721 was numerically the highest standard trolleybus operated by London Transport. Allocated originally to West Ham, it moved to Edmonton in 1954 and to Hammersmith in 1956. P1 1721 has offloaded its last passengers and will turn left into Longmead Road which was the terminal point for 630s only going as far as Tooting. Thankfully for the many would-be passengers, one or both of the two trolleybuses behind are going through to Mitcham and West Croydon. (Tony Belton)

Hammersmith depot had different schedules on Mondays, Wednesdays and Fridays (as opposed to Tuesdays and Thursdays) to accommodate 'punters' attending Greyhound racing at Wimbledon Stadium. Eight journeys were operated before the events and six afterwards. Carrying out a trip to SUMMERSTOWN before the event F1 743 picks up a good load at Tooting Broadway on Friday 8th July 1960. A large number of passengers are waiting at the stop on the other side of the road for transport home. (Peter Mitchell 15402)

Only a few minutes were given for the trips between Tooting Broadway and Summerstown, so conductors had to be quick to get all the fares in before and after the events. Staff had to wind through many displays to find BROADWAY TOOTING when returning from SUMMERSTOWN so the latter panel was left up going both ways; it is unlikely that an inspector will pull staff up for this. 1706 heads away from Summerstown. (Clarence Carter)

For its final fifteen months, 1325 was allocated to Hammersmith depot with much of its time being on the 630, its main service. On 15th June 1960, K2 1325 is at SUMMERSTOWN which was the bottom display on Hammersmith blinds. (Clarence Carter)

Summerstown was not only used for 'Dog Specials' but also for late running 630s from the north. Illustrating this feature, P1 1700 moves from Garratt Lane into Wimbledon Road on the last day of the 630 – Tuesday 19th July 1960. (Jack Gready)

661 is one of a few F1s that spent their last year at Hammersmith depot. 661 is at the junction of Garratt Lane with Wimbledon Road on 1st August 1958 and only going to Shepherds Bush Green on the 630. (Peter Mitchell 11554)

K1 1076, on the 628, is at the junction of Garratt Lane and Wandsworth High Street on 16th July 1960. The Clapham Junction inspector would have noticed that 1076 was running late and instructed the crew to curtail at SHEPHERDS BUSH GREEN. Note the Metropolitan police sign stating 'NO RIGHT TURN EXCEPT TROLLEY BUSES'. (Peter Mitchell 15479)

505 was allocated to Wandsworth depot in 1937; its first seven years were spent solely on route 612. This post-war view sees 505 adjacent to conduit tram track in York Road, Battersea. Another characteristic of its stay at Wandsworth was that it only ever carried Charlton produced blinds. Trolleybuses were only minor players at the depot and during the time that trams and trolleybuses operated simultaneously, trams received better maintenance. Having been transferred to Walthamstow depot on 30th September 1950, D3 505 was retired on the last day of 1952. She, and a number of other D3s were indirectly replaced by new Q1s at Isleworth – some of their C1s went to Walthamstow, allowing the worst of the former Wandsworth vehicles to be withdrawn.

At Battersea, 612s turned right from Battersea Park Road into Candahar Road and then right again into Cabul Road where most drivers parked; return was via York Road. On 2nd July 1950, the driver of D3 511 has parked in Candahar Road – maybe he and his mate want a few minutes rest away from passengers! 511's running number is white on black.

To cover for the work they were given on route 630 in April 1944, three D2s were allocated to Wandsworth depot; however, they were more commonly seen on the 612. Standing in Cabul Road at Battersea is D2 474. The running number is black on white. (Don Thompson)

One of the most dismal termini on the London trolleybus system was Clapham Junction where vehicles on three services stood in Grant Road. Route 626 ran in peak hours only and worked from here to Acton Market Place; due to late running 1202 has been curtailed to only run as far as Craven Park one evening in the summer of 1960. Behind, 1707 also works on the 626. (Don Lewis).

Route 628 is exemplified by D3 532 on the stand with the crew probably having a cup of tea in the nearby café. Stonebridge depot had a daily allocation on the route. (John L Smith)

The 655 service is illustrated by F1 668 which is about to carry out what is the longest possible journey on the London trolleybus system – Clapham Junction to Acton Vale. There were three possibilities as to which via points to show on these trips – 668's conductor shows the more informative one. (John L Smith)

At the junction of Falcon Road with St John's Hill at Clapham Junction, K1 1071 is on a routine trip on route 628 to Harlesden Craven Park. Having spent most of its life at Edmonton depot and working as far north as Waltham Cross, its transfer to Hammersmith in April 1959 saw it working as far south as West Croydon. (Don Lewis)

F1 662 has just started its trip from Grant Road on route 628 and takes on a good load of passengers at the bottom of St John's Hill. Due to increasing private car ownership, traffic restrictions are in force as evidenced by a NO WAITING sign. It is July 1960 and by the year's end trolleybuses would be a transport mode of the past here. (Don Lewis)

Hammersmith was stocked with D class vehicles from 12th September 1937; they stayed there until April 1959 when they were ousted by newer ones. D3 536 is in Wandsworth High Street on 15th August 1954 working on route 628 to Craven Park. (Clarence Carter)

On 2nd June 1957, the Southern Counties Touring Society hired Q1 1891 – the highest numbered trolleybus in the fleet – for an exhausting tour of the system. Having negotiated the 'southern' railway bridge in Putney Bridge Road, 1891 is on its way to Carshalton depot. Behind is D2 477 working on route 630. (John L Smith).

780 was taken out of service at Wood Green depot on the night of 26th April 1960. Due to a vehicle at Hammersmith depot failing, it was sent there the following month. Going only to Shepherds Bush Green on the 630, H1 780 turns from Putney Bridge Road into Putney High Street. (Tony Belton)

It is 3rd October 1960 and trolleybuses only cross Putney Bridge at peak hours now. On the centre of the bridge 692 heads back to Hanwell on route 655; F1 692 has only a month to go before withdrawal. She is in good company – three RT type buses. (Peter Mitchell 16300)

At 8.51am on Monday 11th July 1960, the photographer came across two trolleybuses stranded at Fawe Park Road in Putney Bridge Road. Moving north, it soon became clear that there was a power failure with crews and vehicles just having to wait where they had come to a halt.

F1 719 is adjacent to Crabtree Lane in Fulham Palace Road; indicating that it is out of service the conductor has put up PRIVATE. An engineer uses the telephone on section box V1107 at 9.33am. (Peter Mitchell 15426)

A bit further on, at 10.07am, P1 1705 is at the head of a number of vehicles. One could say that the line-up is impressive, but to passengers it was very inconvenient. (Peter Mitchell 15427)

A little further back, at Niton Street, at 10.33am, the same nine stranded vehicles seen on the previous page make an intriguing vista with their 'sticks' on the wire. 723 is the last in line. (Peter Mitchell 15428)

The next view was taken at 10.47am; F1 665 has been moved on its traction batteries onto the forecourt of Hammersmith Metropolitan Railway Station to free up road space. (Peter Mitchell 15430)

Three minutes later, at 10.50am, Q1 1788 is the first of four vehicles parked up at Hammersmith terminus. It is very likely that the crews are patronising a local café. (Peter Mitchell 15431)

Inspectors have held a trio of trolleybuses on the right-hand side of Butterwick lay-by; this allows motorbuses to pass through freely. F1 663 was due to run through to Clapham Junction; it is now 10.54am and once power is restored the crew will be instructed to take it back to Hanwell – no point going to Clapham Junction! (Peter Mitchell 15432)

Moving west, and outside Goldhawk Road Station, 1865 is at Cathnor Road while 1830 and 1863 have come to a halt at Devonshire Road in Chiswick High Road. (Peter Mitchell 15434, 15437)

Further west, 694 is stranded at Kew Bridge Road Gasworks at 11.35am; the vehicle still shows Clapham Junction; with the last trip to that location being a little over three hours earlier the crew relax and get paid for doing so! In Boston Manor Road at 11.45am F1 708 is the first of three trolleybuses still stranded; third in line is a learner. (Peter Mitchell 15440, 15442)

Other views show that the 660 and 666 were also delayed. When the 'juice' came back on, services suffered from long gaps for quite a time as vehicles and crews had to get back to their respective timings. This was probably the last time that Hammersmith staff experienced such an incident. It is not known how wide an area or how long the delay was (at least three hours) but there would have been a lot of 'passenger grief' about the situation.

The Hammersmith depot routes were prone to late running; at the top of Fulham Palace Road the Hammersmith inspector dashes round to 1085's driver to discuss the situation. The conductor isn't very good at his job as this is not a 628 but a 626 working to Acton Market Place. Mr E. Blazey has his newsagent shop well positioned; bus stops outside shops were good for business. (Tony Belton)

In the spring and early summer of 1960, overhead wiring alignment continually changed to meet revised road layouts at the top of Fulham Palace Road, Hammersmith. When this view was taken, only the 655 operated in the vicinity; F1 683 is about to turn left into Fulham Palace Road on its way to Clapham Junction. 683 is adjacent to Riverside bus garage, and the driver gives the primitive fencing a wide berth. (Tony Belton)

1853.—ROUTE No. 628—WHIT-MONDAY.

Notice to Inspectors and Conductors—Wandsworth Depot.

On Whit-Monday certain Route No. 628 trolleybuses will operate from Wandsworth Depot.

A farebill is exhibited in the depot and must be closely studied.

When running to and from Wandsworth Depot fares will be charged and tickets punched as for St. John's Hospital.

Destination Blinds must be set as follows :—

When Running.	Front and Rear.	Side Blind.
Clapham Junction	8 { Clapham Junction via Harlesden	Wandsworth Putney 3 { Hammersmith Shepherds Bush Harlesden
Scrubs Lane	12 { Nr. Willesden Junction via Putney	
Wandsworth Depot	2 { Wandsworth Depot	—

1855.—ROUTE No. 628 TO OPERATE ON WHIT-MONDAY.

Notice to Inspectors and Conductors—Hanwell Depot.

On Whit-Monday certain Route No. 628 trolleybuses will operate from Hanwell Depot. A farebill is exhibited in the depot and must be carefully studied.

Tickets.

Route No. 655 tickets will be supplied for use when running between Hanwell Depot and Hammersmith Broadway and Route No. 628 tickets for use during the service journeys.

Destination Blinds.

Special blinds containing the required wording will be used and the following destinations must be shewn :—

When Running to	Front and Rear.	Side Blind.
Clapham Junction	8 { Clapham Junction via Harlesden	Wandsworth Putney 3 { Hammersmith Shepherds Bush Harlesden
Scrubs Lane	12 { Nr. Willesden Junction via Putney	
Hammersmith	3 { Hammersmith Broadway	
Hanwell Depot	1 { Private	

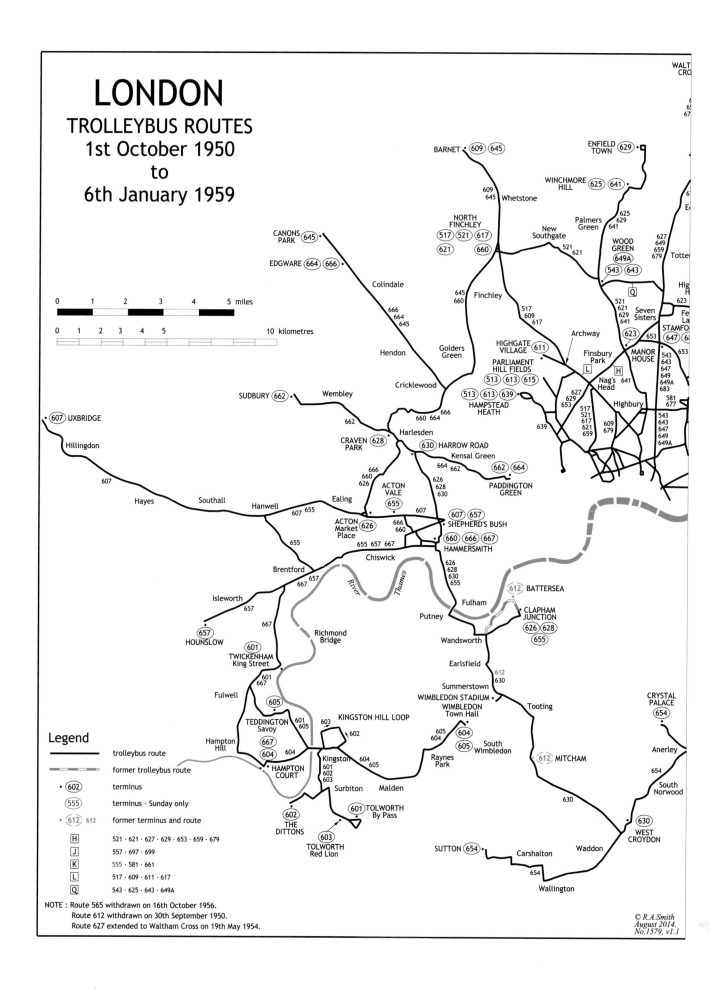

LONDON
TROLLEYBUS ROUTES
1st October 1950
to
6th January 1959

BARNET · 609 645

ENFIELD TOWN 629

WINCHMORE HILL 625 641

CANONS PARK 645

609 645 Whetstone

NORTH FINCHLEY
517 521 617
621 660

Palmers Green

625 629

WOOD GREEN
649A
543 643

EDGWARE 664 666

Colindale

627 649 659 679 Totte

666 664 645

645 660 Finchley

521 621

Q

High F

521 621 629 641 Seven Sisters

517 609 617

STAMFO
647 6

Hendon

Golders Green

HIGHGATE VILLAGE 611

Archway

653

SUDBURY 662

Wembley

Cricklewood

PARLIAMENT HILL FIELDS
513 613 615

Finsbury Park

L

MANOR HOUSE

653

543 643 647 649 649A 683

660 664 666

513 613 639

Nag's Head

H

641

UXBRIDGE 607

Hillingdon

662

HAMPSTEAD HEATH

639

627 629 653

581 677

Highbury

HARLESDEN

660 664

CRAVEN PARK 628

630 HARROW ROAD

Kensal Green

639

517 521 617 621 659

609 679

543 643 647 649 649A

607

Hayes

Southall

Hanwell

662

Ealing

666 660 626

607 655

664 662

626 628 630

662 664

PADDINGTON GREEN

ACTON VALE 655

ACTON Market Place 626

666 660

607

607 657 SHEPHERD'S BUSH

655

655 657 667

660 666 667

HAMMERSMITH

655

Brentford

Chiswick

626 628 630 655

Isleworth

657

River Thames

Putney

612 BATTERSEA

Fulham

CLAPHAM JUNCTION

657

667

Richmond Bridge

Wandsworth

626 628

HOUNSLOW 657

601 TWICKENHAM King Street

Earlsfield

612 630

655

Fulwell

601 667

605

Summerstown

WIMBLEDON STADIUM
WIMBLEDON Town Hall

Tooting

CRYSTAL PALACE 654

TEDDINGTON Savoy

601 605

603

KINGSTON HILL LOOP

602

605 604

604

605 South Wimbledon

612 MITCHAM

Anerley

Hampton Hill

667

604 604

Kingston

604 605

Raynes Park

654

South Norwood

HAMPTON COURT

601 602 603

Surbiton

Malden

630

630 WEST CROYDON

602 THE DITTONS

601 TOLWORTH By Pass

603 TOLWORTH Red Lion

SUTTON 654

Carshalton

Waddon

654

Wallington

Legend

———	trolleybus route
▬▬▬	former trolleybus route
· 602	terminus
555	terminus - Sunday only
· 612 612	former terminus and route
H	521 · 621 · 627 · 629 · 653 · 659 · 679
J	557 · 697 · 699
K	555 · 581 · 661
L	517 · 609 · 611 · 617
Q	543 · 625 · 643 · 649A

NOTE : Route 565 withdrawn on 16th October 1956.
Route 612 withdrawn on 30th September 1950.
Route 627 extended to Waltham Cross on 19th May 1954.

© R.A.Smith
August 2014.
No.1579, v1.1

0 1 2 3 4 5 miles

0 1 2 3 4 5 10 kilometres

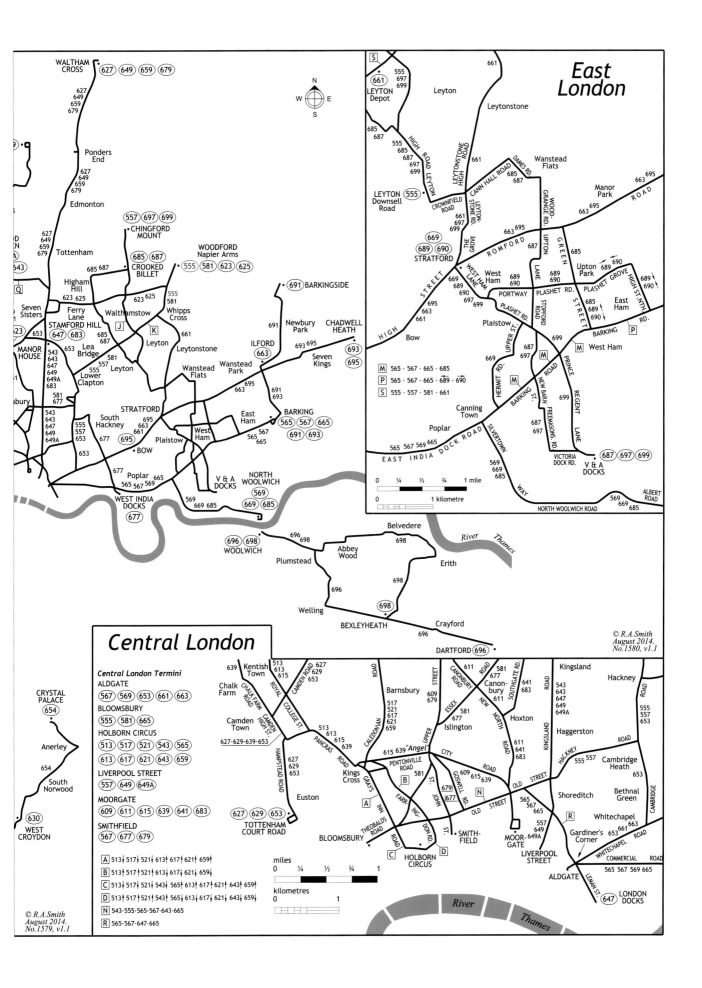

East London

Central London

Central London Termini

ALDGATE
567 569 653 661 663

BLOOMSBURY
555 581 665

HOLBORN CIRCUS
513 517 521 543 565
613 617 621 643 659

LIVERPOOL STREET
557 649 649A

MOORGATE
609 611 615 639 641 683

SMITHFIELD
567 677 679

A 513↓ 517↓ 521↓ 613↓ 617↓ 621↓ 659↓
B 513↓ 517↓ 521↓ 613↓ 617↓ 621↓ 659↓
C 513↓ 517↓ 521↓ 543↓ 565↓ 613↓ 617↓ 621↓ 643↓ 659↓
D 513↓ 517↓ 521↓ 543↓ 565↓ 613↓ 617↓ 621↓ 643↓ 659↓
N 543·555·565·567·643·665
R 565·567·647·665

© R.A.Smith
August 2014.
No.1579, v1.1

© R.A.Smith
August 2014.
No.1580, v1.1

LONDON TROLLEYBUS TRANSPORT

WIMBLEDON & HAMPTON COURT — ROUTES 604
WIMBLEDON & TEDDINGTON — 605

FARES

ORDINARY SINGLE FARES SHOWN IN BLUE. WORKMAN RETURN FARES SHOWN IN RED

All tickets available on day of issue only

Route 604

Stage Point No.														
32	WIMBLEDON TOWN HALL													
31	1½ 3	Darlaston Road												
30	1½ 3	1½ 3	Arterberry Road											
29	2½ 3	1½ 3	1½ 3	Raynes Park Station										
28	2½ 3	2½ 3	1½ 3	1½ 3	West Barnes Crossing									
27	4 4	2½ 3	2½ 3	1½ 3	1½ 3	Shannon Corner or Beverley Road								
26	4 4	4 4	2½ 3	2½ 3	1½ 3	1½ 3	Malden Road							
25	5 5	4 4	4 4	2½ 3	2½ 3	1½ 3	1½ 3	Wellington Crescent						
24	5 5	5 5	4 4	4 4	2½ 3	2½ 3	1½ 3	1½ 3	Kingston Sports Ground					
23	6 6	5 5	5 5	4 4	4 4	2½ 3	2½ 3	1½ 3	1½ 3	Norbiton Church				
22	6 6	6 6	5 5	5 5	4 4	4 4	2½ 3	2½ 3	1½ 3	1½ 3	Eden Street, Clarence Street			
21	7 7	6 6	6 6	5 5	5 5	4 4	4 4	2½ 3	2½ 3	1½ 3	1½ 3	Home Park Gates, Hampton Court Road		
20	7 7	7 7	6 6	6 6	5 5	5 5	4 4	4 4	2½ 3	2½ 3	1½ 3	1½ 3	Paddock Gates, Hampton Court Road	
19	7 7	7 7	7 7	6 6	6 6	5 5	5 5	4 4	4 4	2½ 3	2½ 3	1½ 3	1½ 3	HAMPTON COURT

WHEN RUNNING

24	HAMPTON COURT								
23	1½ 3	Paddock Gates							
22	1½ 3	1½ 3	Home Park Gates						
21	2½	1½	1½ 3	Hampton Wick Station					
20	2½	2½	1½ 3	1½ 3	Holmsdale Road				
19	4	2½	2½ 3	1½ 3	1½ 3	Teddington Lock			
18	4	4	2½ 3	2½ 3	1½ 3	1½ 3	Station Road or Church Road		
17	5	4	4 4	2½ 3	2½ 3	1½ 3	1½ 3	Princes Road	
16	5	5	4 4	4 4	2½ 3	2½ 3	1½ 3	1½ 3	FULWELL DEPOT

Transfer fares

Change at Hampton Court

2½D. Ordinary Single

(20) Hampton, The Thames Riviera &
(22) Eden Street, Clarence Street

4D. Ordinary Single

(18) Hampton, Uxbridge Road &
(22) Eden Street, Clarence Street

Children's fares

DIRECT JOURNEYS ONLY

One child under 3 years of age accompanied by a passenger and not occupying a seat is carried free.

Additional children under 3 years and all children of 3 years and under 14 years are carried at half the adult single fare, fractions of 1d. being charged as 1d. except in the case of the 2½d. adult single fare where the child's fare is 1½d.

Route 605

Stage Point No.																	
32	WIMBLEDON TOWN HALL																
31	1½ 3	Darlaston Road															
30	1½ 3	1½ 3	Arterberry Road														
29	2½ 3	1½ 3	1½ 3	Raynes Park Station													
28	2½ 3	2½ 3	1½ 3	1½ 3	West Barnes Crossing												
27	4 4	2½ 3	2½ 3	1½ 3	1½ 3	Shannon Corner or Beverley Road											
26	4 4	4 4	2½ 3	2½ 3	1½ 3	1½ 3	Malden Road										
25	5 5	4 4	4 4	2½ 3	2½ 3	1½ 3	1½ 3	Wellington Crescent									
24	5 5	5 5	4 4	4 4	2½ 3	2½ 3	1½ 3	1½ 3	Kingston Sports Ground								
23	6 6	5 5	5 5	4 4	4 4	2½ 3	2½ 3	1½ 3	1½ 3	Norbiton Church							
22	6 6	6 6	5 5	5 5	4 4	4 4	2½ 3	2½ 3	1½ 3	1½ 3	Eden Street, Clarence Street						
21	7 7	6 6	6 6	5 5	5 5	4 4	4 4	2½ 3	2½ 3	1½ 3	1½ 3	Hampton Wick Station					
20	7 7	7 7	6 6	6 6	5 5	5 5	4 4	4 4	2½ 3	2½ 3	1½ 3	1½ 3	Holmsdale Road				
19	8 8	7 7	7 7	6 6	6 6	5 5	5 5	4 4	4 4	2½ 3	2½ 3	1½ 3	1½ 3	Teddington Lock			
18	8 8	8 8	7 7	7 7	6 6	6 6	5 5	5 5	4 4	4 4	2½ 3	2½ 3	1½ 3	1½ 3	TEDDINGTON, SAVOY		
	WHEN RUNNING																
18	8	8	7	7	6	6	5	5	4	4	2½ 3	2½ 3	1½ 3	1½ 3	Station Road or Church Road		
17	9	8	8	7	7	6	6	5	5	4	4 4	2½ 3	2½ 3	1½ 3	1½ 3	Princes Road	
16	9	9	8	8	7	7	6	6	5	5	4 4	4 4	2½ 3	2½ 3	1½ 3	1½ 3	FULWELL DEPOT

1246/3477DX/40 paper. Waterlow & Sons Limited, London & Dunstable Route 604/605 January, 1947.

WEST LONDON

THE WIMBLEDON ROUTES

Trolleybuses were first seen at Wimbledon when route 4 commenced on 2nd September 1931; the terminus was in St George's Road which was just short of the main part of the town – an extension to Wimbledon Town Hall occurred on 15th December 1932. Route 4 became route 604 in the summer of 1935 and in May 1940 was joined by the 605; these routes headed through Raynes Park and Malden to arrive at Kingston which was reached on 15th June 1931. The town became the hub of the routes that started under the auspices of the London United Tramways and over the following few weeks, trolleybuses would be seen around the Kingston Hill loop, at Tolworth and at The Dittons. All these services were worked from Fulwell depot where trolleybus services in London were inaugurated on 16th May 1931; the first route operated from Twickenham to Teddington. Such was progress that on 2nd September 1931 Wimbledon was reached with a terminus in St George's Road – this was near Wimbledon Hill. On 15th December 1932, the wiring was extended to Wimbledon Town Hall and no more expansion took place under the LUT; with the formation of the London Passenger Transport Board in July 1933, all further trolleybus developments took place under this governing body. Sometime in 1932, route 5 commenced, operating between Malden and Teddington; working only on Saturday afternoons and evenings, it was later to become a full-blooded service between Wimbledon and Teddington. The Tolworth service was extended from the 'Red Lion'

to the Kingston By-pass on 20th September 1933; on much of this section, concrete traction poles were utilised. Under the LUT regime the routes were numbered 1 to 5; London Transport renumbered them 601 to 605 in the summer of 1935. There was also a peak hour 1A which was renumbered 601A; it worked for some years between Tolworth Red Lion and Surbiton.

Two interesting snippets about the earlier years of trolleybus operation: (1) The March 1932 London United Tramways Traffic Circular stated that it had come to management's attention that motormen were adjusting the brakes of trolleybuses on the road. It was stated that this practice was dangerous and was to be discontinued and if any adjustment was necessary, the fitter available at Eden Street, Kingston or Fulwell depot for this class of work must be called (2) In October 1934, a notice was issued to the staff at Fulwell concerning 'Operating trolleybuses in time of fog'. Conductors were to ensure that their bus was supplied with a lamp for piloting, and during dense fog, day or night, pilots would be stationed at fifteen places on this group of routes. In the absence of pilots at any of these points, conductors were to take on this role. They were also to act as pilots at twenty other locations and at all turning circles. Flares would be placed at six points (Hampton Court, Kingston Bridge, Richmond Road/ London Road, Norbiton Church, Surbiton Station and Malden Dip). These routes were the first to use overhead lights during fog and were colloquially known as 'fairy lights'. These were strings of lights positioned between the two sets of running wires at strategic places such as

On 25th June 1939, shortly before World War Two started, 'Father of the fleet', No 1, waits outside Wimbledon Town Hall ready for a trip to Hampton Court on route 604. The driver is in his white summer coat. Isleworth stout is 7d for a large bottle and 1/1d for a flagon. (Don Thompson)

Experimental trolleybus X1 61 takes on a good number of passengers at Wimbledon for a trip to Hampton Court on 26th May 1947; it is likely to leave fully-loaded. 61 has picked up some bumps and scrapes over the years. Note that the cab door opens in a different manner to that normally seen on London trolleybuses. (Don Thompson)

The usual class of trolleybus on routes 604 and 605 between June 1948 and January 1961 were the eight-foot wide Q1s; leaving Wimbledon Town Hall, 1824 works to Hampton Court on route 604. The Pontevedra trolleybus company in Spain paid a modest £500 for the Q1s they purchased from London Transport – 1824 became their 101. Its stomping ground became Pontevedra to Marin and '1824' was available for service until December 1978 (the author drove 101 from Marin to Pontevedra depot one night in April 1978). Its last overhaul in London had been in January 1960; after being painted in Pontevedra colours in 1961, it went for almost eighteen years without another lick of paint. Not only was 1824 the last London trolleybus to operate with an open platform, it was the last double deck trolleybus in the world to operate in this mode. (Lyndon Rowe)

The final class of trolleybus to be seen at Wimbledon was the L3; seen outside the Town Hall on 15th April 1961 is 1521. With the extension of route 605 from Teddington to Twickenham on Sundays from 11th January 1959, two new displays were provided on blinds manufactured thereafter. As blinds were only replaced when necessary some vehicles used a 667 short-working panel – falling into this category was 1521 which illustrates the single line TWICKENHAM. Twenty-three days later 1521 made history when it left Wimbledon Town Hall at about 11.50pm on 8th May 1962; in carrying out this trip it was the last London trolleybus in service.

Roadworks near Raynes Park Hotel on 20th January 1962 prevented 1419's driver from staying directly beneath the overhead; the poles have not only come off the wires, but the nearside boom is bent. Assistance will be needed. There is no curtailment point between here and Wimbledon, so when 1419 gets under way there will be no alternative but to continue to Wimbledon on route 604. In trolleybusmen's parlance, 1419's driver has well and truly 'had 'em off'. (Peter Mitchell 19824)

Flooding under Malden Dip on Sunday 7th August 1960 saw impromptu action by some Fulwell staff; these views illustrate the shenanigans. 1776 is devoid of a driver who has probably gone to see what's to be done about the situation. Staff did not want to finish late so 1809s driver has curtailed himself short of the flooding; he is a man of extreme 'trolleybus expertise' for he turns round in a side street on trolley – normally, a movement such as this would be done on battery. Not prepared to go through the bridge, three Q1s are at a standstill.

Deciding to make a break for it, 1847's driver ploughs through the floodwater and is followed by another brave soul. The flooding was also extreme at Shannon Corner as demonstrated by 1804. The Q1s were fitted with flood-proof motors so the drivers had every confidence in them. All recognisable vehicles are 604s. (Tony Belton)

The second batch of Q1s was split between Fulwell and Isleworth depots; the former had the lower numbered ones, the latter the higher ones. However, Isleworth immediately found itself with a surplus number of vehicles and 1876, having spent just two months working on the 657, spent its next seven and a half years showing its true worth operating on the ever-busy 607. It was transferred to Fulwell in June 1960, being one of twenty four Q1s that worked out of all three former LUT depots. 1876, on route 603, turns from Kings Road into Park Road on the Kingston Hill loop on 21st January 1961. Ten days later it will be withdrawn and soon be off to a new life in Spain. (Lyndon Rowe)

Having spent some time at Finchley depot, 1521 is now at Fulwell and turns from Kings Road into Richmond Road on the Kingston Hill loop on 1st April 1962. As yet, 1521 has yet to be chosen to be London's last trolleybus. Two services operated round the loop – one clockwise and the other anti-clockwise; route 602 operated in anti-clockwise fashion. Between the running wires are lights that indicate to drivers the line of route to be followed in foggy weather. Many blinds broke when they were transferred from Q1s into L3s at conversion stage nine. New ones had to be made quickly; the height and closely spaced numerals of 1521's route blind indicate this. This blind is safe and sound having been purloined on the last run. (Peter Mitchell 20169)

The Q1s were vastly under-used on backwater routes 602/603; passenger loadings never warranted the use of these magnificent vehicles on them. This view was taken one Sunday morning in January 1961 in Clarence Street Kingston with 1811 having just passed under a section breaker; on the corner of Cromwell Road is Kingston Kinema. 1811 will not work on route 603 much longer as she will be off to sunnier climes in northern Spain the following month; the Pontevedra trolleybus company will be her new owners. (Tony Belton)

L3s replaced Fulwell's Q1s at stages nine and ten of the conversion scheme; this was due to the Q1s going to Spain. Having looked after their Q1s very well, the Fulwell maintenance staff did a good job bringing the vehicles that came from Highgate depot into presentable condition (the Finchley ones that came later were in good repair). To alleviate complaints from drivers about draughty cabs, the ventilators were plated over. The 'new look' is exemplified by 1408 on route 601 and 1432 on the 603 turning into Eden Street at Kingston on 16th August 1961. (Jack Gready)

1444 is at Anglesey Road, Tolworth at 9.37am on 26th February 1962; it is running into Fulwell depot on route 601 so maybe road conditions have enforced a curtailment. Even though it is daytime, all 1444's interior and exterior lights are switched on. (Peter Mitchell 20006)

L3 1523 approaches the centre of Surbiton while working on route 601 to Tolworth; feeder pillar 1306 assists with power supply in the area. Just beyond 1523 are the remnants of what at one time was a complete circle of overhead – it had fallen into disuse by the time that L3s were in the area. According to the Surbiton clock tower it is 1.55pm. (Courtesy Simon Butler)

Having worked at West Ham and Highgate depots in the past, 1399 is now at Fulwell; at 6.39pm on 8th May 1962 she leaves Tolworth Red Lion loop for Richmond Park on route 603. Halting to let 1399 out is another L3 which is on the 601. The following day, both will be parked in the Stanley Road entrance of Fulwell depot waiting to be picked up by Mr Cohen's employees. (Peter Mitchell 20763)

When Fulwell's Q1s were replaced by Highgate's L3s, their staff made a good job of sprucing up these shabby vehicles. 1412 looks good as it turns out of Tolworth Red Lion loop to head for Richmond Park on route 603. (Don Thompson)

curves throughout the system and acted as guides to drivers. They were switched on by an official or conductor when necessary and were switched off when no longer required or after the last trolleybus at night. They were also switched on when light was poor.

Few people can recall travelling on 'Diddler' trolleybuses. Fortunately, Gerald Mead does remember riding on these old-timers and his experiences on them and journeys to school on route 667 are related below:

"My formative years were in Twickenham where, in the early post-war period, buses and trolleybuses played a dominant part in the road-scene; LT, ST, STL and 2RT2 were the standard type of motorbus. The trolleybuses were of two very different species. Route 601 was worked solely by the 'Diddlers' which looked very ancient in comparison to the C1s used on the 667. I travelled spasmodically on the 'Diddlers' as once a month from about 1947, my parents visited friends in Tolworth; we would board a 601 at Twickenham and travel to the Red Lion. My impression was that they were quite good for acceleration but as a passenger I found them very noisy. The lack of handrails in the saloon was very noticeable and passengers had to do the best they could to keep their balance as they made their way to and from their seats. Despite the vehicles being on their way out, the deep cushioned seats were kept in remarkably good condition. Suddenly, in June 1948, bigger and newer vehicles arrived – Q1s. When one turned up, I thought to myself "What's this – something new?" It looked better internally as it had glorious new green seating and the lighting was far brighter in the saloons. They were six inches wider and seated fourteen more than the 'Diddlers'; this solved seating capacity problems in peak hours. The accompanying photographs show the difference between the two types of vehicles. However, there was still a noisy drumming noise from upstairs when the trolley booms went over junctions. In comparison to motorbuses, I observed that the wheels and tyres made a lot of noise in wet weather but they were much quieter and faster than their predecessors. In the transition period I noticed that the 'Diddlers' were very slow compared to the Q1s. Once the 'Diddlers' were gone there was a joint period of C1/Q1 operation at Fulwell. In 1952 the remaining C class trolleybuses were taken off and replaced by more brand new Q1s.

I attended a school at Hampton for six years and always boarded FW5 or FW6 on route 667 at Twickenham. As stated above, C1s worked the route, with 166 being the vehicle I remember the most – I'm not sure why this is but it just sticks in my mind. Other vehicles used on the 667 and which I rode on from time to time were 1565A, 1587A, and 1671 which was a four wheel front drive vehicle. It had a very peculiar interior layout downstairs in that over the front wheel arches, there were seats for three each side – the rest of the seating was of standard design. The 601 and 667 were very busy routes; conductors used TIM ticket machines which had a dial like a telephone on the top and were used by Fulwell and Hounslow depots – I never saw one of them break down. The only time that the punch and ticket system was seen on the 667 was when Hanwell operated a Bank Holiday Monday service between Hampton Court and Shepherds Bush.

Trolleybuses were reliable and I only recall two problems on them. 1) I am sure it was the fault of the crews and not the vehicles for occasionally there was a dewirement at the frog where the 601 and 667 divided in Hampton Road. 601s needed the frog to be pulled – for some reason it remained set for the 601 despite there being a signal light stating which track the frog was set for. Staff tended not to notice this with the resultant 667 suffering 'poles off wires'. 2) A vehicle might be changed-over in Fulwell depot yard; this was a novelty as it was London Transport property and schoolchildren were not allowed access. During my school days, loadings on trolleybuses were very high in peak times; due to the volume of passengers, a 601 would sometimes delay a 667 and we would have to rush to get into school on time. We were late about once a fortnight; however, the master accepted the excuse of "Trolleybus was late Sir."

Having left school in 1953, my contact with trolleybuses became peripheral and to my shame I have to admit that I was unaware of the changeover of Q1s to older L3s in early 1961; my last ride in a trolleybus was probably visiting my parents' friends in Tolworth sometime in the 1950s. My strongest memory of London trolleybuses is the stark change between the 'Diddlers' and the sleek eight foot wide Q1s – what a difference internally and externally."

To summarise, the situation at the end of 1952 with regard to trolleybus services in Kingston was as follows: Route 601 worked between Twickenham and Tolworth – the 602 to The Dittons and the 603 to Tolworth Red Lion both operated around the Kingston loop. Route 604 worked between Hampton Court and Wimbledon with the 605 operating between Teddington and Wimbledon; on 11th January 1959 it was extended to Twickenham on Sundays – this was the last route extension or alteration of any kind on the London trolleybus system. The original stock used on these services were the 'Diddlers' and three experimental vehicles (61–63); most were worn out by the end of the Second World War and replacements in the post-war period were eight-foot wide Q1s. There was little motorbus competition on the routes serving the Kingston network of routes.

None of the 'Kingston routes' were extremely busy; in fact the only time that heavy loadings occurred was on the 604 on summer weekends and Bank Holidays when people flocked to Hampton Court. Crossing the River Thames at Kingston Bridge a non-stop run was usually experienced between there and Hampton Court, drivers giving exhilarating speeds on this stretch. Trolleybuses played a very important part in service provision for the attractions at Hampton Court which was a focal point for a summer's day out. As many crews and vehicles as possible were provided, with London Transport having to rely on staff working overtime so as to get people home on the busiest days. At Hampton Court, the 604 connected with the 667 which was one of two routes forming stage one of the tram to trolleybus conversion (27th October 1935). Routes 604/605 crossed the River Thames at Kingston; the winding course of the river meant that the 667 paralleled it near Hampton. The 667 worked between Hampton Court and Hammersmith Broadway and was operated by Fulwell depot which used standard vehicles; occasionally a 'Diddler' would be pressed into service on the route. Q1s followed, though down-trodden L3s replaced them in early 1961 bringing a rather neglected air to the somewhat salubrious areas of Hampton Court, Kingston, Tolworth and Wimbledon.

The fateful day has arrived: Tuesday 8th May 1962 and 1386 on the 601 is in the 'trolleybus only lane' adjacent to the Kingston By-Pass. The bus stop flag had been on the concrete traction standard; in anticipation of new services the following day, a new bus stop pole and flag have been positioned adjacent to it. However, the flag on the traction pole that serves bus routes using the by-pass has yet to be re-sited. (Tony Wright)

It is 24th June 1961 and L3 1400 is a relatively recent addition to Fulwell's fleet – this was not a popular move as downtrodden L3s replaced the ever-popular Q1s earlier in the year. Note the concrete traction standard; these poles were synonymous with the Tolworth loop – in the background is the Kingston By-Pass. (Peter Mitchell 18118)

On 19th October 1957 Q1 1769 speeds along Portsmouth Road towards THE DITTONS; there are two reasons why it shows 601 rather than 602: (1) an inspector has commandeered a 601 to cover a gap in the service (2) a conductor shows the wrong route number. The destination blind does not incorporate a VIA before SURBITON – these blinds were made at Chiswick Works who normally only manufactured motorbus blinds so they are 'doing their own thing'. 1769 was exported to Spain in 1961 and operated between Coruna and Carballo; the second rate road surface between the two towns meant that 1769's condition rapidly deteriorated. A far cry from what she was used to when working from Fulwell depot. (Peter Mitchell 10455)

There was no quieter terminus than THE DITTONS which was served solely by route 602. L3 1519 waits there on 17th March 1962. The QUEUE THIS SIDE sign is irrelevant as only a few passengers are likely to board at any one time. (Peter Mitchell 20094)

1852 heads for Twickenham on route 601 during its last days of service with London Transport. It crosses the River Thames at Kingston Bridge, and as the sign on the left indicates, is leaving the Royal Borough of Kingston on Thames. The advertisement for the Sunday Telegraph details the launch of its first issue of February 5th 1961 by which time 1852 will have been withdrawn; in fact she moved to Poplar garage on February 3rd. (Fred Ivey)

A link wire at Kingston Bridge enabled vehicles to move from Hampton High Street into Hampton Court Road. It saw limited service operation but was useful if Fulwell engineers wanted to give a vehicle a long test run. At the start of the link, 1519 takes up service from Fulwell depot working on route 602 to Richmond Park. (Jack Gready)

With no other vehicle in sight, 1799 on route 605 turns at Teddington Post Office. Until 1959 the loop had been described on blinds as TEDDINGTON SAVOY; with the closure of this cinema, a new designation was applied. Sold to the Pontevedra trolleybus company, this vehicle was broken up for spares – you are in your last days 1799! (Lyndon Rowe)

The Stanley Road end of Fulwell depot, along with tram tracks disused since 1931, is seen on 21st October 1951. Some traction poles have their lower parts painted white to assist staff – it is not known why some have been painted and others not. The mid-thirties building is on the right; on the left a vehicle is at the entrance to the overhaul works. (John Gillham)

The largest task ever undertaken in Fulwell Works was the altering of a large number of vehicles from half cab to full cab layout; their bulkheads were strengthened at the same time. In November 1937 a D2 and two C2s are receiving professional treatment from skilled workers. The device in the foreground is a folding guillotine and rolling machine for sheet metalwork. (London Transport Museum U25242).

1788 is at the junction of Stanley Road and Hampton Road while working on route 667 to Hampton Court; a 601 and another 667 can be seen. The trailing frog outside 'The Nelson' is an access link between the two entrances of Fulwell depot. (Tony Belton)

1441 has just passed the facing frog on the south side of Kingston Bridge and is outside the 'Old Kings Head'. It is unlikely that any stops will be made between here and Hampton Court so the driver can have 1441 flat out on top notch all the way. Route 604 was one of seven services that formed the final stage of the conversion programme. The inside set of wires are a link between Hampton High Street and Hampton Court Road. This view was taken on 14th April 1962 – just twenty four days to go now! (Peter Mitchell 20270)

It is 14th August 1939 and declaration of the Second World War is imminent. Everything is tranquil now though as A1 24 waits at the Hampton Court terminus of route 604. Isleworth Stout was prolifically advertised in West London.

Q1 1856, works as FW 4 on route 604 to Wimbledon; it has just left Hampton Court stand and is about to circle the roundabout. Breweries and distilleries were regular advertisers on London trolleybuses with Guinness and Haig competing with each other here. (Fred Ivey)

On August Bank Holiday Monday 1960 (7th August) Hanwell were only able to provide three trolleybuses (rather than eleven) on the 667 service between Shepherds Bush and Hampton Court. Crews worked to inspectors' instructions that day; 709, 712 and 1784 all showed EXTRA rather than 667. Q1 1784 leaves Hampton Court for Shepherds Bush – it can just be discerned that a 667 display is shown in the side box. (Fred Ivey)

1876 is in Hampton Court Road on the last stretch of its journey from Shepherds Bush. The conductor has elected to display a 657 route number which was contrary to instructions – they were supposed to show 667 on the way to Hampton Court. (Ron Wellings)

Trolleybus Routes
3790
Hammersmith or Shepherds Bush and Hampton Court

Operation from Hanwell Depot on Bank Holiday.
Notice to Inspectors and Conductors, Fulwell and Hanwell Depots.

On Easter Monday certain trolleybuses will operate from Hanwell Depot between Hammersmith and Hampton Court, and Shepherds Bush and Hampton Court.

1. **Fares and Tickets** (Hanwell Depot)
   A farebill for Route 667 is exhibited in Hanwell Depot when running between Half Acre, Brentford and Hanwell Depot. Fares will be charged as on Route 655 and the present farestage point numbers will be used.
   When running between Hammersmith or Shepherds Bush and Hampton Court farestage point numbers as shown on the Route 667 farebill will be used. In order to conform to the practice on T.I. Machines used at Fulwell Depot, conductors will punch tickets in the farestage and point number at which the passenger boards the trolleybus.

2. **Route Nos.:**
   When leaving Hampton Court for Shepherds Bush—Show Route No. 657.
   When leaving Hampton Court for Hammersmith—Show Route No. 667.
   When running to Hampton Court—Show Route No. 667.

3. **Destination Blinds** (Hanwell Depot).

When Running to	Show		
	Front and Rear		Side
	No. Wording	No.	Wording
Hampton Ct.	25 Hampton Ct. via Brentford & Twickenham		
Hammersmith	26 Hammersmith Broadway via Twickenham and Brentford	9	Chiswick Kew Brentford Twickenham Hampton
	27 via Twickenham and Brentford Shepherds Bush		

Punch type Special Cheap Return tickets used by Hanwell depot on route 667 on Bank Holiday Mondays.

It is 7.22pm on 27th May 1960 and a number of Q1s have run into Fulwell depot after the evening peak. Those with their poles on the wires, on the left, have entered via Wellington Road – identified are 1812 and 1819. Those on the right have come in from Stanley Road – 1843 and 1784 are in view. Out of service with its poles dropped is 1769. Later on they will be cleaned, washed and put to bed on the appropriate lyes in the depot. Note the road numbers on the depot wall – two to twelve can be seen. (Peter Mitchell 14669)

2.45pm Tuesday 8th May 1962 and District Mechanical Engineer Bob Brown nudges 'Diddler' No 1 to the Wellington Road entrance of Fulwell depot. An inspector armed with a bamboo pole will swing its trolley booms from one set of wires to another so that it can move onto the public highway and off to Twickenham. No. 1 is participating in a ceremonial trip and has a full load of VIPs on board; 1521 in the background, taking on the lesser mortals, will follow it. A number of trolleybus staff watch the goings-on and a couple of schoolgirls have accessed the forecourt. (London Transport Museum U23698)

The 'Diddler' is now in Wellington Road and Bob Brown will take his foot off the power pedal as it passes under a section breaker. In front of No 1 are a film crew who made a film titled 'Route 601'; despite many enquiries, it has never come to light. The car on the left has a CD registration – maybe an enthusiast from the Brighton area has driven up for the occasion. A vicar witnesses the historic event. (Mike Abbott)

From Twickenham the trip then proceeded to Kingston via route 601; the two vehicles then travelled around the Richmond Park loop via route 602 to conclude near Kingston Bus Station. Ken Tuddenham was the driver of 1521 which leaves Twickenham with a police escort; on the other side of the road a tower wagon was provided in case problems arose – none did. (Peter Moore)

Following the 1958 bus strike the Kingston routes received heavy cuts in service levels; to reduce the impact on the 601, route 605 was extended from Teddington to Twickenham on Sundays from 11th January 1959. L3 1399 has been out on the road for some time and waits on Twickenham stand; sister vehicle 1497 has just come out of Fulwell depot and needs to get in front of 1399. The driver of 1497 uses a bamboo pole to switch the trolley arms to the outside set of wires. (Peter Moore)

Bill Tuddenham was a driver at Fulwell and was later promoted to inspector. His son Ken joined London Transport in 1955 as a conductor at Fulwell and became a driver in 1958. At that time Fulwell was stocked with Q1s which were six inches wider than standard vehicles. 'They were a joy to work on' summarises Ken who now relates his own 'round London by trolleybus'.

"Fred Nutting was my driving instructor – he was a well-respected man and knowledgeable about all things trolleybus; he was one of the few full-time instructors (most were drivers acting up in this capacity). He had been on the job for years, having been a former London United Tramways man. When I did my training there was just another conductor and myself making up a 'school'. We soon became familiar with driving a trolleybus and the wiring around routes operated by Fulwell, Hanwell and Isleworth depots (the former LUT area); we also went down to Clapham Junction which was on Hanwell's 655 route. Fred said to us one day, "Let's go up to Woodford". Neither myself or the other chap had any idea where it was and had never been there before – I've never been there again either! We got to Woodford alright and on the way back (at Walthamstow, Bell Junction) Fred said to me, "Drop the poles Ken" and the next minute my colleague is driving the trolleybus down to Walthamstow depot on battery power. We thought it was lunchtime but Fred was a sly old fox as this was his first port o' call to see some of his colleagues – he was a leading figure in the sports and social side of London Transport and I was to find out in the next few days that he was using the tuition trolleybuses for his own purposes!. We get out of Walthamstow and the next thing we're heading up through Tottenham and Edmonton – a Q1 must have looked very strange up there. Soon we're in Ponders End bus garage, this time only for a cuppa as the motorbus side of things was not in Fred's jurisdiction. Once we're out of the garage we battery the trolleybus around a corner and end up at Waltham Cross; we didn't stop as we needed to get back to Fulwell.

Next day it's "We'll have a day out today" and from Hammersmith we find our way to West Croydon. Soon we're amongst the oldest trolleybuses in the fleet (the B1 class) and we end up in Carshalton depot where we have a meal break and Fred sees his friends. When we leave the depot we get back to Croydon and fully expect to follow the 630 wires back to Hammersmith; no, Fred's got other ideas. "Keep going" he says, and we find ourselves manoeuvring around twists and turns on the narrow streets north of there. Eventually we arrive at the bottom of Anerley Hill. "We can't go up there" Fred says "we haven't got run-back brakes", so we have to turn on a reverser that I now know was at Versailles Road. We make our way back to Fulwell, asking him why he's taken us round Norwood and Selhurst. His reply was that he wanted us to get used to all types of traffic conditions and types of road that may face us. On another occasion we went up to Enfield, but later on when we arrive at Lea Bridge depot to see his colleagues, we're not allowed to take the vehicle onto the premises as a Q1 is too wide to enter – we left the vehicle, poles down in Lea Bridge Road. The 'jewel in the crown' came one day when there are two driving schools going on and Fred arranges with the other instructor for us all to go over to Bexleyheath. Only Fred knew how to get there but as he seemed to know all the overhead junctions in London it was a relatively easy task. We got ourselves onto the Commercial Road in East London when suddenly we're told "Turn left here" and we're soon in Poplar depot.

The two trolleybuses used were 1779 and 1842; these were the first of the 1948 and 1952 batches of Q1s and were commandeered straightaway for driving training duties at Fulwell and Isleworth depots respectively. There wasn't time for a cup of tea at Poplar and two instructors and four trainees all bundle onto 1779, leaving 1842 in Poplar (many years later, these two vehicles were back there pending shipment to Spain). We get to North Woolwich where the poles are pulled down. To our amazement, Fred then gets into 1779's cab, puts it into battery mode and drives the thing onto the North Woolwich free ferry; there we are being paid for having a ride on the river! We get to the other side, up go the poles and before long we're at Bexleyheath depot where again Fred sees his mates and we have a lunch break. We retrace our steps to Poplar to retrieve the abandoned 1842. By the time we get back to Fulwell, it's time to pack up for the day.

I passed my driving test first time and was issued with badge T7436 (I lost it in 1960 and was given a brand new one – T14283). I was put on the spare roster for three weeks and was loaned to Hanwell depot on one occasion. I was given a spreadover duty on route 607 (that meant working in both peak hours with the time in between being paid for); this service ran between Uxbridge and Shepherds Bush which I'd gone over on driver training. The depot staff had to ensure that I was given a Q1 on both spells of duty; it would have been no good giving me one of the F1s as I'd no experience with the regenerative brake that they were fitted with.

I liked working on trolleybuses and having a position at Fulwell depot; my father related an intriguing incident when he was on duty in Kingston. A motorbus driver was transferred to Fulwell (which was unusual in itself) and a few days after passing his test, was going westwards through the town. Still thinking that he was driving a motorbus, he tore through the junctions at great speed. Dad saw that a potential catastrophe was about to occur and that some of the junction might easily drop to the roadway. Putting his hands on his head, he dived into a shop doorway to avoid whatever might fall to the ground. Amazingly, nothing happened and the driver just sailed through and passed over Kingston Bridge none the wiser for his lapse of concentration. My dad was a stickler for rules and wanted staff to wear their caps – there was no favouritism for me but about 300 yards after I passed him I would take my cap off! Fulwell depot had a big works attached to it, and sometimes I would go in there to see what was going on.

Pay was okay but only good if extra work was done – overtime or rest day working. In 1958, matters came to a head over pay and on Sunday 4th May everything ran as normal; however, the public had been beefed up by the press that an all-out strike would start the following day. There wasn't any hostility towards us and in general the public were sympathetic to our cause. The trolleybuses ran in that night, and after cleaning had their poles dropped and electrics switched off. The only concession made that night was for the staff trolleybus to take crews home; this duty just did its first half – two trips to Kingston and Twickenham with the crew just getting paid for the short time that they were at work. Once it got into the depot, the big green doors were pulled to; it looked really strange seeing them fully closed – this was the only time I saw this. The 'inside' staff had a hard job closing them as it had been a long time since they had done this (the maintenance staff were not involved with the dispute and came in for work as normal). As the trolleybuses could not be moved easily, there was little they could do apart from cleaning and moving a few vehicles into the maintenance area for routine work; their main role was fire-watching – security really. The general hands did little else than keep the depot tidy. The overhead staff did not participate in the strike, but they did go out to check the overhead from time to time.

As May dawned, London Transport was aware that they were in for a long haul and brought into the works by the fourth of the month, a lot of trolleybuses ahead of their scheduled overhaul date. This allowed work to be got on with and meant that there wouldn't be too big a backlog when the dispute was over. Of course the works could only take so many vehicles and by Tuesday 13th May the staff had completed everything they were supposed to do and became victims of a 'lock-out'. However, to avoid any confrontation, they were told to go home and would get full pay. The works staff were brought in by staff buses from various parts of London; these vehicles were kept at various garages, but with the start of the strike they were entombed so could not get to Fulwell. The works staff had to make their own way there and did this by giving and getting lifts, or travelling on the suburban railway to Fulwell station. The same situation occurred at Aldenham and Charlton works; vehicles were brought in early for overhaul and when staff ran out of work they were sent home on full pay.

London Transport was hoping, right up to the last minute that the strike would be avoided. They were in the business of running buses and at the time of high staff shortage, needed to keep the recruitment momentum maintained. Therefore they were taking on staff almost until strike day. London Transport didn't terminate their employment as they wouldn't come back when the strike was over. The conductors were kept at Chiswick Works and had classroom and on-bus instruction using RT training buses running around the premises; the recruits acted as members of the public. There was no recruitment during the strike period and potential drivers who had been taken on had an easy seven weeks doing nothing much else than drink cups of tea in Chiswick canteen; intriguingly, there was only one conductor coming to Fulwell – when he eventually arrived, he was a 'know-it-all' who was soon put in his place! At the time, we had three conductors who were driver-training at Fulwell. As they were members of the union they didn't work; when they restarted their training they had to go over to Colindale to complete it (punishment!). One of our drivers was at Chiswick at the time, training for his PSV badge – this would allow him to drive motor buses on staff private hires. He had to pack it in when the strike started and go back and finish it at London Transport's convenience. I availed myself of this facility and obtained my PSV badge in 1960, two years ahead of the rest of the drivers at the depot.

Word soon got round that the strike had been called off on Friday 20th June and that day the depot was opened up and we went in to find out our shifts for the following day – we picked up the duty that we would have worked had the strike not taken place. Once the engineers knew that the strike had been called off, they placed the trolley poles on the overhead; this charged up batteries and built up air pressure (presumably engines were started at bus garages). The next day everything ran out as normal. The trolleybuses went straight back into service with the same carbons in the trolley heads that they had run in

with almost seven weeks previously. The power was kept on during the strike as London Transport was concerned about overhead being stolen. In fact a notice was placed on the depot forecourt stating 'Power is on'. This drew the matter to the staff's attention but also acted as a deterrent to metal thieves.

There was one fact that affected trolleybuses and not motorbuses; drivers were concerned about muck that had accumulated on the running wires during the dispute. Not only were we anxious about the general state of the overhead, but we were also worried about the filth and any litter that had blown into the troughing under bridges. We were told that a couple of trolleybuses had been out cleaning wires the preceding night (Thursday 19th June) – presumably London Transport sensed an ending of the strike and gave instructions for some wire cleaning – maybe at all depots. We were informed that Twickenham, Teddington and the Kingston area had been done but not the distant parts – Hammersmith and Wimbledon. We asked for ice-cutting skids to be fitted to the trolley heads of the first trolleybuses going there so that the overhead would be clean; this was refused on the basis that they were only fitted in frosty weather and that 21st June didn't qualify. As it was summertime though, there was little flashing and arcing from the dirty overhead; even the Brentford Half Acre loop didn't take too long to become polished as 655s/657s turned there regularly.

I hadn't driven a trolleybus for several weeks and when I first got into one, everything seemed a bit strange; as an example, I'd forgotten the order of the positions of the switches that controlled the lights and windscreen wipers; after a couple of minutes in the yard though I became used to everything again. Everybody was glad to get back to work; as we'd all lost a lot of money during the dispute, we did a lot of overtime and rest day working to make up for it. The management made the most of this and were able to cover all of the duties for many weeks afterwards.

In April 1954, London Transport announced that the trolleybus system was to be scrapped – however, accountants would have asked some very embarrassing questions if the Q1s were withdrawn after such a short life. Therefore it was stated that Fulwell and Isleworth depots were to retain them until they were life expired, probably in the late 1960s. At this time Fulwell had the lower numbered Q1s with the higher ones at Hanwell and Isleworth.

The trolleybus conversion programme started in March 1959 and by the end of the year four stages had been completed. Fulwell was not involved in any of this; to us, conversion to motorbuses was not an option – we didn't come into the equation. However, there had been enormous financial benefits and London Transport decided that they would get rid of the rest of the trolleybuses and that a fourteenth stage would be added to the programme. The news of this soon filtered back to us and there was a general air of despondency about it all for we were very happy on trolleys. The drivers considered the Q1s to be the 'Rolls-Royces' of the trolleybus fleet; conductors liked working on them as there was so much room for them to go about their duties – the travelling public appreciated them too. There was nothing we could do so we just had to enjoy them for their remaining time with us. It was a sad announcement for drivers, conductors and maintenance staff. What we didn't realise was that the Q1s were going to be taken away long before we changed over to motorbuses; it was not until December 1960 that the TGWU were advised that they would be withdrawn in the first few months of 1961 and that we would receive older trolleybuses from North London depots.

Drivers had to be trained on the electric brake and 1449 was brought over from Finchley depot for the job; our painter had an obsession of putting an FW code on any trolleybus that operated from the depot and he put one on each side of 1449. It took a long time to train us all up but everybody was dealt with by changeover night which was Tuesday 31st January 1961. It was chaos in the depot as all but eleven of our Q1s were taken away and replaced by sixty four L3s from Highgate. They all had their blinds left in so they had to be removed; similarly the Q1 blinds had to be taken out and put in the replacements. There were blinds all over the depot floor; the Q1 blinds had been in the vehicles for up to ten years and had become brittle – some split at the slightest touch. Consequently there weren't enough blinds to go round and some vehicles were despatched the next day with handwritten boards – in the chaos some blinds went in upside down! A very bad impression was given to the travelling public on the Wednesday. The situation was a bit less tense with fare charts – out with the Highgate ones and in with those from the Q1s.

As many as possible of the Q1s were put in the Works; the rest were left in the depot which didn't matter as they were all off to Poplar bus garage in a few days' time as they were being shipped to Spain (following the Hanwell conversion in November 1960 twenty had departed in the first few days of 1961). While all this was happening there were still two Q1s being overhauled in the Works – 1766 and 1768; what a waste of money. What was also supposed to occur that night was the movement of twenty-two Q1s to Isleworth with a corresponding number arriving at Fulwell withdrawn. This would have made the whole situation impossible so the changeover was made beforehand. By 14th January Q1 1862 was with us and I drove some of the higher numbered Q1s – not 1891 though the highest numbered trolleybus in the fleet. Although our maintenance staff made sterling efforts to keep the former Highgate trolleybuses presentable, they could never get them up to the same standard as the

Q1s. Our final eleven Q1s were taken out of service on Tuesday 25th April 1961 and replaced by eleven L3s from Finchley. Though we missed the Q1s, at least we did have trolleybuses for another year or so – but it just wasn't the same. The L3s were in a deplorable state and initially an embarrassment; the cabs were too cold so the coachmakers plated over the ventilators. The maintenance staff gradually got them into a presentable condition

On the final day of London trolleybuses, I was working early turn on the Kingston routes. Having finished my duty I returned to the depot where I was commandeered by one of the depot inspectors and asked if Barbara Reid (my conductress) and I would like to crew a ceremonial trolleybus that afternoon – the DIs had forgotten to cover the work and it was a last minute job to find somebody to do it. Many of the bigwigs were going to be around so a white cap had to be found for me as I didn't normally use one. 1521 was assigned to the job; however, it suffered a bad dewirement in the depot when they were preparing it for the run and the maintenance staff had to be scrambled to repair a bent boom. It was only because special posters had been fitted that 1521 was used and not another one. Having sorted the problem out, 1521 was put into position behind the 'Diddler' which was the lead vehicle in the 2.45pm departure from Fulwell depot; the 'Diddler' was being driven by Bob Brown, the Divisional Mechanical Inspector. Leaving the yard we went to Twickenham then to Kingston via Teddington; round the Richmond Park loop and back to Kingston bus station. We had to take 1521 back to the depot but I went via Hampton Court (where we had a cup of tea) as it would take longer. Eventually we got back to Fulwell. I went home and had a rest but I did go and see 1521 close the London trolleybus system about 1.45 the following morning. Routes 601 to 605, 657 and 667 were the last trolleybus services; their final day was Tuesday 8th May 1962.

Having left London Transport I went to Doncaster and drove buses there. I was one of a number of drivers with the South Yorkshire PTE who had a licence for 'trolley vehicle' and participated in trolleybus trials there in the mid-eighties".

"On Sunday 15th April 1962, I drove one of two trolleybuses used for a tour of the remaining routes for the PSV Circle. The vehicles were 1425 and 1526 – I drove the latter. Both have been parked by 'The Nelson' public house which is at the junction of Stanley Road and Hampton Road. I am walking away from 1526."

BRENTFORD TO HOUNSLOW

A fascinating feature of the 667 was an Easter, Whitsun and August Bank Holiday Monday service working between Shepherds Bush and Hampton Court; not only did Fulwell participate but Hanwell and Hounslow also joined in. Flagrant breaching of Ministry of Transport regulations took place on these occasions, for to reach the 667 wires at Brentford, the eight foot wide Q1s that Hanwell often put out on the route, travelled along Boston Road which was banned to trolleybuses wider than seven foot six inches. Hanwell's conductors had individual ways of displaying a route number for this service; some put up EXTRA while others showed 657 or 667. The Hanwell destination blind displays for these outings were not always used correctly and all manner of permutations could be seen. This eleven vehicle service was run in addition to the ordinary 667; Hanwell last operated on this unadvertised service on August Bank Holiday Monday 1960. To partly compensate, a much boosted frequency was provided for August Bank Holiday Monday 1961; many only ran as far as Brentford Half Acre but with many using the route between there and Hampton Court, good loads were carried. Although Fulwell could have worked the Shepherds Bush to Hampton Court service that year, no thought was given to continue it. Isleworth dropped out of these workings by the mid-1950s meaning that their crews only worked the 657; seemingly boring, it meant that the staff knew everything about the route like the back of their hands.

Also starting on 27th October 1935 was route 657; operating between Hounslow (Wellington Road) and Shepherds Bush it was worked by Hounslow depot which was renamed Isleworth in July 1950. Original provision, as with the 667, was with seventy-seater C1s. Replacements came in the form of Q1s in the summer of 1952; with their sale to Spain in 1961, K1s operated in their place. Having been kept in good condition at Wood Green depot, this state of affairs happily continued at Isleworth. The 657 and 667 connected at Busch Corner Brentford, where 'friendly rivalry' took place between staff on the two routes. Eastbound 657 crews would halt at the stop before Busch Corner hoping to see trolley arms of a 667 appearing above a woodyard situated there; similarly, 667 crews would look over the woodyard to see if they could espy a 657's trolley booms. The winner was the crew with the greater will power! Whoever went first carried the load; this could be significant as there were some notable places between there and Youngs Corner – Syon Park, Kew Bridge and London Transport's Works at 566 Chiswick High Road. Westbound from Busch Corner, the 657 was on its own to Hounslow with the 667 only having a short overlap in the Twickenham area (with the 601) as it made its way to Hampton Court. Good loads were carried by the 667 when international rugby matches took place at Twickenham.

As already stated, the 657 was operated by Isleworth depot with eight foot Q1s; their staff referred to the seven foot six wide vehicles at Hanwell as 'narrow 'buses'. Isleworth driver, Tony Shanny was driving his 657 beneath the Chiswick flyover one day when he came across a 655 which had dewired at the roundabout there. The 655 conductress was trying to rewire the vehicle with a bamboo pole, but being a small woman was having a real struggle. She and her driver had had a row earlier in the day and he refused to get out of the cab to sort things

Isleworth was stocked with the higher numbered vehicles of the 1952/53 batch of Q1s; due to the convolutions involved in their sale to Spain in 1961, they were replaced by Q1s of 1948/49 vintage at stage nine of the conversion scheme. Representing the new order, 1832 passes through Busch Corner on its way to Hounslow on route 657. (Sid Hagarty)

TIMES OF FIRST AND LAST TROLLEYBUSES
Route 657
SHEPHERDS BUSH & HOUNSLOW

FROM	TO	MONDAY to FRIDAY		SATURDAY		SUNDAY	
		First	Last	First	Last	First	Last
		morning	night	morning	night	morning	night
Shepherds Bush	Kew Bridge	5 20	12 11	5 20	12 5	8 30	12 7
	Busch Corner	5 20	12 11	5 20	12 5	8 30	12 7
	Hounslow Depot	5 20	12 11	5 20	12 5	8 30	12 7
	Hounslow (Wellington Road)	5 20	12 11	5 20	12 5	8 30	11 51
Seven Stars	Shepherds Bush	5 14	12 4	5 14	11 58	8 23	12 0
	Kew Bridge	5 25	12 16	5 25	12 10	8 35	12 12
	Hounslow (Wellington Road)	5 25	12 16	5 25	12 10	8 35	11 56
	Hounslow Depot	5 25	12 16	5 25	12 10	8 35	12 12
Young's Corner	Shepherds Bush	5 10	12 0	5 10	11 54	8 19	11 56
	Kew Bridge	5 29	12 50	5 29	12 48	8 39	12 16
	Busch Corner	5 29	12 50	5 29	12 48	8 39	12 16
	Hounslow Depot	5 29	12 50	5 29	12 48	8 39	12 16
	Hounslow (Wellington Road)	5 29	12 20	5 29	12 14	8 39	12 0
Kew Bridge	Shepherds Bush	5 1	11 49	5 1	11 44	8 9	11 45
	Busch Corner	5 41	1 1	5 41	12 58	8 49	12 27
	Hounslow Depot	5 41	1 1	5 41	12 58	8 49	12 27
	Hounslow (Wellington Road)	5 41	12 31	5 41	12 24	8 49	12 11
Busch Corner	Shepherds Bush	4 51	11 40	4 51	11 34	8 0	11 36
	Kew Bridge	4 51	12 16	4 51	12 14	8 0	11 36
	Hounslow Depot	5 50	1 10	5 50	1 8	8 58	12 36
	Hounslow (Wellington Road)	5 50	12 40	5 50	12 34	8 58	12 20
Hounslow Depot	Shepherds Bush	4 46	11 34	4 46	11 28	7 55	11 30
	Kew Bridge	4 46	12 10	4 46	12 8	7 55	11 30
	Busch Corner	4 46	12 10	4 46	12 8	7 55	11 30
	Hounslow (Wellington Road)	4 29	12 46	4 29	12 40	7 39	12 26
Hounslow (Wellington Road)	Shepherds Bush	4 39	11 27	4 39	11 21	7 48	11 23
	Kew Bridge	4 39	12 3	4 39	12 1	7 48	11 23
	Busch Corner	4 39	12 3	4 39	12 1	7 48	11 23
	Hounslow Depot	4 39	1 3	4 39	12 57	7 48	12 36

SERVICE INTERVALS	MONDAY TO FRIDAY	10-20 minutes until 6 a.m., then 4-6 minutes until 8 p.m., then 8-12 minutes.
	SATURDAY	5-15 minutes until 7 a.m., then 4-6 minutes until 8 p.m.; then 8-10 minutes.
	SUNDAY	10 minutes until 10.30 a.m., then 8 minutes until 12.45 p.m. ; then 5 minutes until 7 p.m. then 8 minutes.

CHANGE AT YOUNG'S CORNER FOR TROLLEYBUSES TO HAMMERSMITH.

ON PUBLIC HOLIDAYS services run at special times which are advertised in the vehicles.

ALL ENQUIRIES TO LONDON TRANSPORT, 55 BROADWAY S.W.I.   ABBey 1234   6   .11.39.

39—18570—Proof. Post between Shepherds Bush and Young's Corner and between Busch Corner and Hounslow.   Waterlow & Sons Limited, London & Dunstable

Chiswick Works supplied a number of blinds for Fulwell and Isleworth depots in the post-war years; motorbus practice saw them use L.T. GARAGE as an amplification. Continuing this practice, 1886 shows ISLEWORTH L.T. DEPOT as it stands on the forecourt on April 24th 1955. Q1 1886 has yet to be overhauled; in fact it will only receive one overhaul while working in London. Isleworth depot was the sole operator of route 657. (Peter Mitchell 7113)

At the time that this view was taken on 30th December 1959, it was intended that the trolleybus services operating out of Fulwell and Isleworth depots would continue until the late 1960s/ early 1970s; this was due to their routes being operated by Q1s. There is no foreboding at the present time, but soon a decision will be made to abandon the rest of the trolleybus system at the end of the original scheme. The Q1s were offered for sale and a purchasing mission from Spain saw all but two exported. 1866 waits outside Isleworth depot, working west to Hounslow on the 657. Although crew changes occur here throughout the day, both bus stops are request. (John Clarke)

Shaw of Isleworth skies his trolleys when leaving the depot on Saturday 29th April 1962. Shaw looks on disconsolately as his conductor gets to work with a bamboo pole to re-wire 1126 so that it can get on its way to Hounslow on route 657. At the time, Terry, you said to me, "Don't let my guvn'r see that". It's more than fifty years on and you're now beyond recrimination; therefore it is time to show this photograph! Terry Shaw was the last man to 'pass out' as a trolleybus driver in London. (Hugh Taylor)

A close-up view of the last man to obtain a licence to drive trolleybuses in London. Terry Shaw stands beside 1117 on Isleworth depot forecourt on 7th April 1962. (Hugh Taylor)

It is the last day of trolleybus operation in London and 1057 has just passed 'The Bell', Hounslow on the final lap of its trip from Shepherds Bush to Hounslow on route 657; the driver has already changed the blind for his next eastbound trip. Going the other way is an RT on route 117 which will replace the 657 the following day. In the evening, 1057 will dewire under Isleworth Station bridge and require the attendance of the Fulwell breakdown gang – this was the system's last call-out. (Tony Wright).

A quirk that manifested itself in the last few weeks of the London trolleybus was the pairing of newly qualified driver Adrian O'Callaghan, with long-serving conductor George Clark. Adrian was issued with badge number T14898 and George had T1300. This meant that the highest numbered driver's badge was working with the lowest numbered conductor's badge; they would not have known the significance but the photographer did! On 28th April 1962, they stand in front of 1274 at the Hounslow terminus of route 657. K1 1274 became the last Leyland trolleybus to operate in the United Kingdom when it entered Isleworth depot a few minutes into 9th May 1962. (Hugh Taylor)

K1s soon settled into life working between Hounslow and Shepherds Bush on route 657; at the Wellington Road terminus at Hounslow, 1144 waits for departure to 'The Bush' on 17th March 1962. The '1' of the EXV 144 registration had faded over time and was never dealt with by the Isleworth painter. (Peter Mitchell 20086)

Traffic Signals. Method of Operation for Trolley-buses.

Hounslow Trolleybus Terminus.

When trolleybuses are due to leave the lay-by, the Conductor must press the push button fixed on Pole No. 368. There is also a white light fixed on this pole and Conductors must wait for the " All clear " light before signalling drivers to proceed.

Drivers must not leave the lay-by until receiving the signal to do so from the Conductor.

A minimum of 14 seconds and a maximum of 15 seconds is allowed for vehicles to proceed from the lay-by and enter into the Eastbound flow of traffic.

On the traction pole next to 1144 is a button that conductors can press when trolleybuses were about to depart. This set the traffic lights at the junction of Wellington Road with Staines Road to red, allowing a free path for eastbound 657s. This facility was still serviceable on 19th May 1962 – the author pushed the button and the accompanying photograph shows the illuminated light. (Hugh Taylor)

F1 668 crosses the Great West Road while working on route 655 to Hammersmith on 5th November 1960 – this location was known locally as MacLean's Corner; the building in the background is the Beecham Research Laboratories. Crawford's Cream Crackers adverts were seen on many London trolleybuses; 668 will be withdrawn three days later. (Tony Wright)

The only place of note between Brentford and Hanwell was Boston Manor where a station on the Piccadilly Line was situated. Heading towards Hanwell Broadway on route 655 on 26th August 1960, F1 718 descends the slope of the bridge. The majority of the hundred strong F1s were at Hanwell all their lives – most were there at the end of services too. (Peter Mitchell 15841)

out – this was unfair as it was his fault that the 655 was in this predicament. Tony got out of his cab and rewired the vehicle which then got on its way; he often travelled part of his way to work on a 655 and sometime later came across the same clippie who was now with a different driver. He enquired whether this man was now her regular mate; she said he was and had got rid of her previous driver in spectacular style. On their next late turn after the flyover incident, he had wanted to get a ride home on the last westbound 607; this meant running into the depot a few minutes early. When the trolleybus arrived outside the depot, she pulled the frog handle down but before the booms passed through the frog, let go of the handle. She dived into the depot to pay in, leaving him to sort out trolley arms splayed across Hanwell Broadway; he lost his ride home, and they parted company a few days later!

Still in former London United Tramways territory at Shepherds Bush, were four full-time (607, 628, 630 and 657) and one peak hour service (626); this meant a trolleybus in sight virtually all the time here in 'traffic hours'. The overhead layouts were constructed so that terminating services and through routes did not impede each other. Shepherds Bush was a big interchange point for buses, trolleybuses and the Underground; this hub attracted many shoppers. The nearby Hammersmith was a focal point of trolleybus operation with seven routes.

Route 655 started on 13th December 1936, operating between Hammersmith and Acton Market Place via Brentford and Hanwell; a peak hour extension saw it reach Harlesden Craven Park. The Sunday service only worked between Hammersmith and Hanwell, but as there were no turning facilities at Hanwell at the time, for its first four months it turned at Hanwell, Hospital Gates which was opposite Hanwell (later Southall) bus garage. With the introduction of the 626/628/630 in September 1937, the opportunity was taken to push the 655 through to Clapham Junction; the Craven Park concept was simultaneously withdrawn.

The 655 reached its greatest extent in July 1946 when it was extended at its northern end in peak hours to Acton Vale, Bromyard Avenue; at 14.8 miles it was London's longest trolleybus route. The 630 was measured at 14.65 miles, little more than the distance between the bottom of Falcon Road and the terminus at Grant Road, Clapham. It would be interesting to know how London Transport was able to measure these distances to within 265 yards. The two longest routes in London, the 630 and 655, ran beside each other between Wandsworth and Hammersmith. Road traffic impeded trolleybus operation in the mid-1950s and the number of journeys operating the whole length of the route was gradually reduced until from October 1959 there were just three morning peak hour journeys running in one direction, Clapham Junction to Acton Vale. By now, the 655 was only working to Clapham Junction in Monday to Friday peak hours; in fact at these times the route was virtually operating in two sections: Acton Vale to Brentford and Hanwell to Clapham Junction. Due to parallel bus and trolleybus services, the 655 was not a 'money spinner' and at quiet times it just shuttled between Hanwell and Brentford, Half Acre – there were other services on this stretch with the only place of note being Boston Manor.

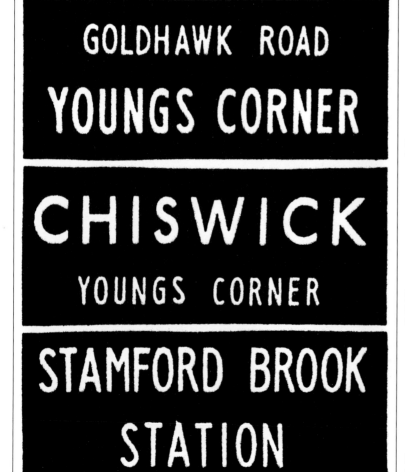

Initial destination blind panel for turning at Stamford Brook Station for Fulwell and Isleworth vehicles.

Destination panel used at Hanwell depot for a short time to describe the turning arrangements at Stamford Brook Station.

Universal panel used for trolleybuses turning at Stamford Brook Station – used by Fulwell, Hanwell and Isleworth depots.

1779 was the first Q1 to be delivered – 31st January 1948 – and immediately became one of the Fulwell training vehicles. Instructors would take budding drivers around some of the frequently used short-working points so as to familiarise them with the wiring. On 9th August 1960, Q1 1779 is in St Pauls Road on the Brentford Half Acre loop. (Tony Wild).

742's conductor has not made a good job of displaying HANWELL BDY (part of the next display – VIA HORN LANE – can be seen). 742 is adjacent to St Pauls Road from where vehicles short-working to Brentford Half Acre depart. Route 655 was one of three services that travelled through Brentford High Street. This view was taken on 14th May 1960. (Peter Mitchell 14514)

The best of Wood Green's K1s were sent to Isleworth at stage ten of the conversion scheme; their purpose was to replace their Q1s which had been sold to various Spanish operators. 1074 moves from Brentford Half Acre into St Pauls Road on 8th May 1962; a number of afternoon peak journeys on route 657 were scheduled to turn here – this is one of the last to do so. Note the destination blind showing BRENTFORD (HALF ACRE) – there were just a small number of displays on the network which saw the amplifying point bracketed. 1074 was towed to Colindale scrapyard five days later – by the end of the month she had been broken up. (Peter Mitchell 20748)

Isleworth's 1858 passes Kew Bridge station on its way to Hounslow on route 657; behind, another Q1 makes its way towards Hampton Court on the 667. The siding is for vehicles turning at the north side of Kew Bridge; by 1961 it was used very rarely, if at all. In fact the crossover was causing problems so all 'special work' here was removed in February 1962. (Tony Belton)

1823 passes beneath the recently completed Gunnersbury flyover on 14th May 1960. Q1 1823 spent its entire life working from Fulwell depot and would have worked on route 667 to Hampton Court hundreds of times during its career. (Peter Mitchell 14514)

L3 1393 is outside London Transport's Chiswick Works and near the entrance of Gunnersbury station on 27th August 1961. Many of London Transport's employees would have used 667s on their way to and from work here. 1393 is running into Fulwell depot. (Peter Mitchell 18725)

The 667 Bank Holiday service run by Hanwell was additional to the regular 667 operated by Fulwell; examples of both are seen at Youngs Corner on 6th June 1960. Hanwell's 1847, showing 657, is about to turn left into Goldhawk Road while Fulwell's 1787 will carry straight on to Hammersmith Broadway. 1847's driver has placed the timecard on a ledge at the front of the cab – the back of it shows a large **X** over previous details. (Fred Ivey)

K1 1061 spent most of its life in North London; at stage twelve of the conversion scheme it was deemed to still be in good enough condition to act as an engineer's spare vehicle and was sent from Wood Green to Isleworth depot. This was a good move for on 7th February 1962 it replaced its numerical sister 1062 which had received a rear-end shunt; in doing so, 1061 became the last London trolleybus to be re-activated and relicensed. 1061 pulls out of Goldhawk Road into Chiswick High Road at Youngs Corner while working on route 657 to Hounslow.

The last time London trolleybuses encountered snowy conditions was on 26th February 1962. Seen just south of Goldhawk Road Station, K1 1117 heads for Isleworth depot on route 657; it is followed by sister vehicle, 1058, going to Hounslow. (Peter Mitchell 20008)

Due to increasing traffic delays, a circle of wires was erected outside Stamford Brook Station in May 1957 – crews had to swing trolleys to a dead-end wire to get onto the circle. Initially described on Fulwell and Isleworth blinds as GOLDHAWK ROAD YOUNGS CORNER and on Hanwell's as CHISWICK YOUNGS CORNER, uniformity was reached when STAMFORD BROOK STATION was used for all three depots. By 1961, trolleybuses on route 657 were frequently held up by heavy passenger loadings and traffic on Saturdays so often ran a few minutes late; curtailments at Stamford Brook were frequent. 1101 leaves the loop on Saturday 13th May 1961. There are another fifty one Saturdays to go before trolleybuses pass from the London scene. K1 1101 will spend her remaining days on the 657 and work on 'Last Trolleybus Day'. (Peter Mitchell 17273)

In the mid-1950s, a number of E1s moved from West Ham to Stonebridge depot. One was 573 which turns from King Street into Studland Street at Hammersmith; these roads were part of the general one-way system here. Rather than use a display that incorporated a via point for North Finchley, the conductor uses plain NORTH FINCHLEY which was used for 'shorts' from Golders Green. The conductor has wound through the whole blind for this; maybe he/she is new to the job and has yet to memorise the order of displays. (Don Thompson)

Trolleybuses on routes 655 and 667 that terminated at Hammersmith used a one-way system that saw them move from King Street into Studland Street, then along Glenthorne Road and Beadon Road to stand in Hammersmith Grove; return was via King Street. On 3rd October 1960 F1 718, on route 655, is in Glenthorne Road with the conductor having already changed the front blind to HANWELL BDY. Behind is RTL 190 working on route 27 to Kensington. (Peter Mitchell 16304)

Q1 1787 is in Beadon Road and nearing the end of its trip to Hammersmith on route 667; the driver has already changed the destination blind to HAMPTON COURT. Adjacent is RTL 340 on route 27 to Highgate; this is a crew changeover point for Riverside Garage as a driver, and a conductor with his bell punch ticket box under his arm, wait for their vehicle to materialise. (Don Thompson)

1582 turns into Hammersmith Grove where it will have a few minutes time stand before heading for Colindale, its home depot. It is 3rd October 1960 and 1582 has been operating in north and west London for a little over a year now. The middle set of wires is for routes 655/667; the nearside set is for peak hour journeys to Clapham Junction on route 655. (Peter Mitchell 16307)

The snow has yet to abate at 2.35pm on Sunday 31st December 1961 – despite the appalling conditions two 667s have arrived at Hammersmith. This implies that they have somehow been able to keep to time. 1399 is the photographer's subject; 1491 is in front. (Peter Mitchell 19711)

Just five former Wandsworth D3s survived into the late 1950s. One was 504 which is seen outside the Queen Caroline Street entrance to Hammersmith Underground station shortly before the new one-way system was introduced here. 504 is on the long 630 route to West Croydon. (Fred Ivey)

Until 12th July 1958 southbound trolleybuses moved from Queen Caroline Street into Fulham Palace Road where there was a junction that led to Hammersmith depot which is off to the left. In what can only be a peak hour view, 529 on route 626 heads for Acton Market Place while 741 on the 655 proceeds to Clapham Junction; in the background, another 655 on its way to Hanwell. The driver of 529 gives the boy with the handcart a wide sweep. (Norman Simmons)

Butterwick opened on 13th July 1958 as part of the one-way traffic arrangements at Hammersmith. K2 1240 turns into Butterwick while working on route 628 to Clapham Junction on 2nd July 1960, (Peter Mitchell15344)

A long-time resident of Stonebridge depot was 271 which is in Butterwick on route 628 in April 1959. C2 271 sports paper destination blinds in both front boxes. Adjacent to 271 is RTL1384 working on route 27 to Turnham Green. (Fred Ivey)

Stonebridge depot was given some work on route 628 in January 1951; this service was linked with the peak hour 626 and a few journeys were operated by them on that route. C3 286 is on the 626 to Clapham Junction and is in Butterwick in July 1958, shortly after this road was opened. The vehicle is very well presented – the blinds are perfectly positioned and the paintwork shines. (John Boylett).

K2 1201 leaves Hammersmith depot for Harlesden Craven Park on route 628 at 1.25pm on 14th May 1960. The sign above the depot used to read HAMMERSMITH TROLLEYBUS DEPOT; as can be seen, part of it has fallen away. 1201 is in its last days here; it will be withdrawn on the night of 19th July 1960 and go to Colindale to be held as a spare vehicle. Within days it will be relicensed and sent to Stamford Hill to spend its final year there. (Peter Mitchell 14511)

K1 1080 is at the southern end of Shepherds Bush Road on Saturday 16th July 1960 and running into Hammersmith depot on route 628; any passengers on board will have to alight at the next stop – Butterwick. 1080 spent most of its life in North London but the policy of withdrawing the less recently overhauled specimens early in the replacement scheme saw it move to Hammersmith in April 1959 – withdrawal from active service is the following Tuesday night. At stages two, four and six of the conversion programme, some stretches of wiring were retained for emergency use. It would have been worthwhile to have kept the Hammersmith to Shepherds Bush link as there had been times when it had been used for diversionary purposes and for transferring vehicles from one route to the other under the flexible working arrangements that the trolleybus side of London Transport enjoyed. This was not to be and this short section was handed over to Cohen's (scrap merchants) shortly after conversion stage seven. (Peter Mitchell 15474)

On Whit Monday 1960 (6th June) five Stonebridge trolleybuses supplemented the normal Hammersmith 628 allocation. One vehicle working on the route that day, and for the only time in its life, was 1614 which emerges from Shepherds Bush Road into Shepherds Bush. The amplification of CRAVEN PARK was unusual – there were just five examples of this on the system; all are illustrated in this book. This was the last day that a passenger could board a 628 at Clapham junction and purchase a 1/7d ticket to Stonebridge depot. (Fred Ivey)

To provide work for Fulwell crews on Bank Holiday Mondays they worked additionally to Hanwell on the Shepherds Bush to Hampton Court 667 service; this was one of the few occasions that they saw Shepherds Bush. Seen there on 2nd June 1952 the conductor of 1787 (who is using a TIM machine) goes round to have a word with his driver. (Alan Cross)

Shepherds Bush was served by five trolleybus routes; these were withdrawn at three stages of the conversion programme – seven, eight and fourteen. When stage fourteen came round, route 657 was operated by K1s; before this, Q1 1873 rounds Shepherds Bush Green before returning to its home depot of Isleworth. (Fred Ivey)

It was not uncommon for 607s to travel in convoy; they could be delayed by passenger and vehicular traffic. Epitomising this on Saturday 5th November 1960, Q1 1851 leads 716 and 1770 through Shepherds Bush; it is not known whether the fourth vehicle is a 607 or a 657. (Jack Gready).

1784 was one of seventeen Q1s nominated for early withdrawal – this would have occurred at stage eight of the conversion programme. So that they would only receive minimal maintenance, 1784 was one of sixteen Q1s recorded as moving from Fulwell to Hanwell depot on 24th June 1960. Q1 1784 has just left the Shepherds Bush terminus of route 607 on 5th November 1960 with the conductor giving a nominal hand signal to motorists. 1784 ended up in Coruna in Northern Spain – cut down to single-deck. (Jack Gready)

Most of the hundred strong F1s were always associated with Hanwell depot; one was 718 which has just passed under Shepherds Bush station bridge in Uxbridge Road. There were many journeys on the 607 that only worked as far as SOUTHALL DELAMERE RD. The bubble car in the foreground illustrates the small amount of road space needed for parking. (Tony Belton)

At the time that this view was taken – 9th August 1958 – route 655 was working all the way from Acton Vale, Bromyard Avenue to Clapham Junction on Saturdays. It is 1.48pm and F1 670 is just starting the 14.8 mile trip from Bromyard Avenue to Grant Road at Clapham, where it is due to arrive at 3.05pm. (Peter Mitchell 11651)

The last view that the photographer took on Tuesday 2nd January 1962 (conversion stage thirteen) was of N1 1636 turning short in Bromyard Avenue, Acton Vale at 3.35pm. In the background are Government offices. Many of the workers will have used the 660 route over the years – today is the last time that they will travel on one. (Peter Mitchell 19762)

1596 on route 660 turns from King Street into the High Street at Acton on 29th October 1960. The wires leading to the left are for 607s and 655s short-working at Acton Market Place; the wires which 1596 uses are for routes 660 and 666 – the 626 had gone by now. (Jack Gready)

United Dairies were a long-established firm with shops located throughout the capital. Passing the Ealing Common branch on 17th April 1955, F1 699 heads east to Shepherds Bush on route 607. As can be seen, Hanwell depot kept their vehicles in tip-top condition. (Peter Mitchell 7085)

By the mid-1950s, the increasing amount of congestion in West London made it necessary for the long 655 route to be split into two sections in Monday to Friday peak hours: Acton Vale to Brentford, and Hanwell to Clapham Junction. F1 693 is at Ealing Broadway on 7th September 1960 – it is working from Acton Vale to Brentford, Half Acre. (Jack Gready)

The last F1 in service was 733 which is seen in Ealing on its final journey on Tuesday 8th November 1960. It's Hanwell depot now, Fulwell for a single day's storage Wednesday, and make your own way to Mr Cohen's scrapyard behind Colindale depot on Thursday. The driver has considerately held 733 so that the photographer could take this time exposure. (Tony Wright).

K1 1164 had been at Hammersmith depot since stage two of the conversion programme and was withdrawn at stage seven. Six days later it was relicensed and sent to Hanwell to work on routes 607 and 655 until stage eight when it was finally withdrawn. 1164 is seen at West Ealing Park on 30th October 1960. Note the RAC parking sign and a 'Free car park' sign. (Peter Mitchell 16393)

On 26th June 1955, the Southern Counties Touring Society hired B1 66 for a marathon tour of the system. One port o' call was Hanwell depot where 66 is parked alongside one of the native F1s – 723 is about to depart to Hammersmith on route 655. This is a very active scene for a Sunday with numerous members of staff going about their business. A chalked hand-board for the day details cheap fares that had been available on buses and trolleybuses before 1pm. It is 4.36pm and 66 will soon head back to Carshalton depot.

Hanwell depot is seen on its last day of trolleybus operation – 8th November 1960. Q1 1767 is parked, poles down, on the forecourt. Very little indicates that this is the final day; some bricks on the left and a 'Buses for Trolleybuses' poster in one of 1767's nearside windows. (John Gillham)

749, which is HL 7 on route 607, heads west to Hayes End Road; if he hasn't done so already, the driver is about to come off his power pedal as he passes the Hanwell Broadway crossover. Wires to the right are for 655s to Brentford and beyond. (Fred Ivey)

Learner trolleybuses were regularly seen around the system with a number of nominated vehicles being used; the window behind the driver could be removed so that instructors had quick access to the cab if need be. F1 700 is a Hanwell learner and on a rainy 15th April 1959, makes its way down Boston Road; the trainee needs to be familiarised with the 655 wiring. The scrapping programme has just begun and Stonebridge's 189, which had been in store in Hanwell is towed by one of Cohen's wagons to Penhall Road, Charlton for dismantling. 700 has no fears at the present and will continue in service until 8th November 1960; however, the next day will see her stored in Stonebridge depot. The irony is thus: 189 arrived from Stonebridge as a 'live' vehicle – it departs from Hanwell as a 'dead' one. 700 is a 'live' vehicle but leaves for Stonebridge as a 'dead' one. This view was taken on the day that stage two of the conversion programme was implemented. (Fred Ivey)

Crossing the River Brent at Hanwell Bridge at 6.04pm on 29th July 1960, F1 685 is running late. It was common in peak hours for 607s to get held up so an inspector has said to the crew "Hillingdon" – he definitely wouldn't have said "HILLINGDON CHURCH AND STRATFORD BDG!" Aware that they need a bamboo pole to swing booms from the main line to a 'dead-ender' there, the crew will hope a bamboo pole is stowed beneath 685. If not, they'll have to wait until another 607 turns up and use theirs. (Peter Mitchell 15593)

The last Saturday of operation of route 607 was 5th November 1960. Just visible in the background is the Iron Bridge at Southall which takes the Great Western Railway to the west. On its way to Hayes End Road F1 718 picks up and sets down passengers at the request stop after the bridge. (Peter Mitchell 16437)

The Q1s were admirably suited for working on the Uxbridge Road; 1770 is at Parkfield Avenue which is midway between Hillingdon and Hayes End on 5th November 1960. It is using one of the dual carriageways encountered on the western part of route 607. (Peter Mitchell 16426)

 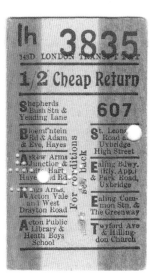 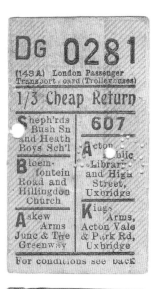

Cheap return tickets used on route 607.

696 was one of many F1s at Hanwell depot that spent much of their lives plodding up and down the Uxbridge Road between Shepherds Bush and Uxbridge on route 607. Many journeys on Mondays to Saturdays only went as far as Hayes End Road where a very smart 696 waits for the conductress to pull the frog handle down for the siding on 15th August 1959. She makes sure that the lady with her child alights safely – or is she thinking 'Get your own pram and child off lady'. (Lyndon Rowe)

Two H1s were sent to Hanwell depot towards the end of May 1960 – 774 and 782. Route 607 ran through populated areas; however, there was a short rural section in Hillingdon where 774 is seen on its way to Uxbridge. (Peter Moore)

The loop at Hillingdon Church was regularly used by late running trolleybuses on route 607; in this instance 1770 carries out such a manoeuvre. The Aldenham blind shop created an erroneous display – instead of reading HILLINGDON CHURCH STRATFORD BDG it stated HILLINGDON CHURCH AND STRATFORD BDG giving the impression that a shuttle service operates between the top and bottom of Hillingdon Hill (Stratford Bridge was a bridge over a small stream just west of here). 1770 turns through the gap in the dual carriageway at the bottom of Hillingdon Hill. (Fred Ivey)

Hanwell built up a sizeable number of Q1s over the years; one was 1854 which leaves the 607 short-working at the bottom of Hillingdon Hill. The leafless trees indicate a winter view. A grit bin states STICK NO BILLS – the similar NO BILL STICKERS slogan was the butt of jokes. (Don Thompson)

29th October 1960 so not long to go for the 607; a 'Buses for Trolleybuses' poster can be seen on the traction standard in the right foreground. 751 is at the bottom of Hillingdon Hill, about to pass over the River Pinn at Stratford Bridge. Despite their age, the majority of the all Leyland F1s continued in service until November 1960 – their general good condition allowed this. (Jack Gready)

A busy Saturday scene on 5th November 1960 sees 1152 halting at the 607 compulsory stop outside Uxbridge Station. Although the loop on the station forecourt was used for a few weeks in 1954 while road works took place between there and the terminus, its use thereafter was spasmodic – just allowing the occasional vehicle out of turn to get in the right order. Haig promote their wares many weeks before Christmas – do the advertising department know that 1152 is due for withdrawal in four days' time? (Peter Mitchell 16410)

108

Uxbridge terminus was situated at Frays Bridge. Sitting silently in the afternoon sunlight on 7th May 1960 are two of the stalwart F1s – 705 and 730; the third of the trio is an unidentified Q1. Time schedule 7803, working with duty schedule 966, required forty-three trolleybuses to operate on route 607 between Uxbridge and Shepherds Bush on Sundays (no Hayes End Roads). The only sign of life is a member of staff behind 705. (Peter Mitchell 14475)

607	Uxbridge & Shepherds Bush	...	M-F.	15	12	15	8	7792	967	Hanwell	66	TB	66	Approved for 8ft
607	Hayes End & Shepherds Bush	...		15	12	15	8							wide vehicles.
607	Southall & Acton Vale	...	...	6	—	6	—							
607	Uxbridge & Shepherds Bush	...	Sat.	10/12	17	17	16½/12	7802	958	Hanwell	68	TB	68	
607	Hayes End & Shepherds Bush	...		10/12	17	17	16½/12							
607	Uxbridge & Shepherds Bush	...	Sun.	10	12	18	20/15	7803	966	Hanwell	43	TB	43	

Before trolleybuses commenced at Hammersmith, there had been a lot of congestion in the area, some of it caused by trams. When the MOT inspector made his report, he stated that the alignment taken by trolleybuses at Hammersmith Broadway should effect considerable improvement in traffic conditions generally. However, with the increase in private car ownership, congestion again reared its head and to alleviate this, a one-way system introduced on 13th July 1958 saw routes 626, 628, 630 and 655 diverted southbound away from Queen Caroline Street to use a new road named Butterwick; this also entailed revised access arrangements for Hammersmith depot.

Route 607, worked between Shepherds Bush and Uxbridge which was the westernmost place that the London trolleybus reached. The 607 was considered by many to be London Transport's most prestigious trolleybus route. Passenger loadings were very high and at its height 607s were passing through Hanwell Broadway at the rate of one a minute in peak hours. Operated by Hanwell depot, the route enjoyed the use of dual carriageways beyond Hanwell, allowing high-speed runs on these stretches. The 607 passed through Southall,

Ealing and Acton; to satisfy demand on its busiest parts, there were many scheduled short-workings – Hayes End Road, Southall Delamere Road and Acton Vale Bromyard Avenue. Apart from a couple of places where bus services joined and left the Uxbridge Road between Hanwell and Uxbridge, the 607 was on its own. D class vehicles were initially used but were not fast enough for the route, so were soon replaced by a hundred higher horse powered F1s. Because passenger use was so heavy, reinforcements were soon sought and some K1s appeared; in January 1953 some Q1s were allocated, enabling the K1s to move out. It was not unusual to see 607s travelling in convoy and once past the Hayes End inspector, drivers would have their vehicles on top notch all the way to Uxbridge where a turning circle was constructed at Frays Bridge. While on the subject of Uxbridge, a turning circle was installed outside Uxbridge Station while roadworks took place at the terminus; it was used from 3rd March to 27th July 1954. The last day of operation of route 607 was 8th November 1960; to cement the fact of it being its most prestigious route, London Transport brought in the most recently overhauled trolleybus – Q1 1812 – to close the service.

Rainy days always slow the traffic so it is no surprise that 1085 is only going as far as FULHAM PALACE RD EDGARLEY TERRACE on route 626 rather than Clapham Junction. Pedestrians wait for 1085 to move out of Wood Lane and into the Uxbridge Road part of Shepherds Bush where it will run round the Green and continue its journey south. The buildings on the left are emblazoned with period adverts: cigarettes, beer, washing powder, milk, etc. (Tony Belton)

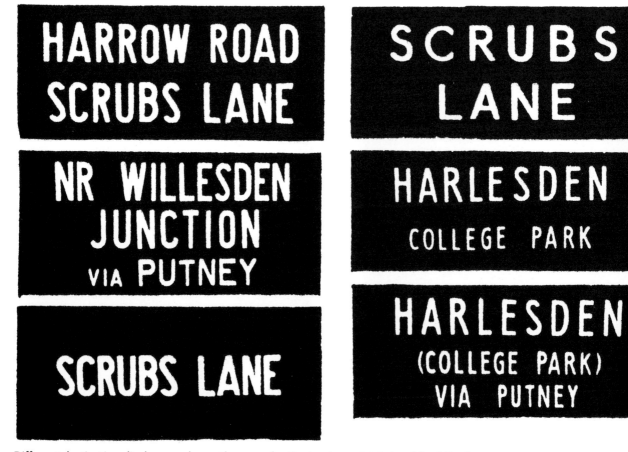

Different destination displays used over the years for the turning point in Letchford Gardens.

464 is seen just south of Shinfield Street (a turning off Wood Lane) at 8.48am on 16th March 1959; it is working the last morning peak hour trip from Acton Market Place to Clapham Junction on route 626. D2 464 looks in magnificent condition, but within a month she will have been taken out of service at Hammersmith depot and sent to Stonebridge for short-term storage before being sent for scrap a fortnight later. This was due to the policy of replacing the older trolleybuses by newer ones in the conversion programme; most of Hammersmith's trolleybuses came into this remit at stage two and were replaced by K class vehicles. (Peter Mitchell 12558)

When Stonebridge depot were given work on route 628 it was on a daily basis; some of the oldest vehicles in the fleet were to be seen on it now. C2 192 (one of a hundred and two vehicles fitted with rear wheel spats) is in Scrubs Lane at its junction with Dalgarno Gardens on March 13th 1955. (Peter Mitchell 6828)

K1 1275 is seen on 14th May 1960 passing under the iron-work of the Scrubs Lane over-bridge while working on route 628 to Clapham Junction. Woe betide any driver who has his poles off here – a lot of damage would occur if metal collided with metal. (Peter Mitchell 14507).

N2 1657 turns from Scrubs Lane into Waldo Road while working on route 662 – it is 7th May 1960, Cup Final day, so the extra number of people in the Wembley area may have caused the late running and necessitated the curtailment. Behind, 1241 is just a minute into its seventy-seven minute trip to West Croydon on route 630. A number of traction poles had a suffix added to them; on the left is pole 4A which reads A4! (Peter Mitchell 14474)

1722.—AUTOMATIC FROG, SCRUBS LANE, JUNCTION WITH WALDO ROAD.

Notice to Trolleybus Drivers and Conductors—Hammersmith and Wandsworth Depots.

The frog at Pole No. 5a, Scrubs Lane, down track, is now electrically operated.

Two push buttons are provided on Pole No. 6, down track, marked " Curve " and " Straight " and an indicator on Pole No. 5, up track, shows the direction for which the frog is set :—

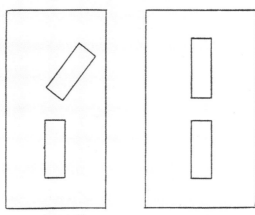

Set for Waldo Road.   Set for straight road.

Conductors of buses turning into Waldo Road will operate push button marked " Curve " ; drivers must not proceed until the indicator shows that the frog is properly set. The frog will be reset for the straight road automatically by trolley skid passing a skate just beyond the frog.

Drivers of buses proceeding towards Harrow Road must not pass the indicator until it shows that the frog is set for the straight road. If not properly set it can be corrected by operating the push button marked " Straight " on Pole No. 6.

EMERGENCY OPERATION.

In the event of the electrical apparatus becoming defective the frog may be operated by means of the emergency pull handle provided. This will be found under the pull frog mechanism on Pole No. 5a and is operated as follows :—

To set frog for Waldo Road.
Pull handle down as far as it will go, approximately 4 inches. (It does not require to be held down.)

To set frog for straight road.
Give handle a sharp tap upwards—this will release it and set frog.

In the event of failure, call for tower waggon.

The northern terminus of route 630 was in Letchford Gardens, Harlesden which for many years was described on destination blinds as NR WILLESDEN JUNCTION. With the introduction of Aldenham produced blinds it became known as HARLESDEN (COLLEGE PARK). 1201 heads a line-up of four 630s and is only going to BROADWAY TOOTING where a number of turns were scheduled. A loop is provided here; strangely though, the frog is set for the inside track – conductors had to pull a frog handle to use the outer one. Note the use of bracket arms; interestingly one of them holds the facing frog equipment. (Don Lewis)

The southern terminus of route 666 was Hammersmith where C3 294 is seen on 15th August 1959; it is running into Colindale depot. The C class vehicles were the staple diet of this route since inception until August 1959 when, as part of the conversion programme, they were replaced by newer vehicles that had been operating in the East End. 294 will carry its last passengers in three days' time – the scrapman beckons! (Lyndon Rowe)

Hammersmith was the starting point for routes 660 and 666. The 660 came into being on 5th April 1936, working between Hammersmith and Acton Market Place. Temporarily withdrawn in July it was re-introduced on 2nd August 1936 running from Hammersmith to North Finchley. The 666 commenced on 5th July 1936 operating from Hammersmith to Edgware; for most of its life it was a peak hour service that only became daily in January 1959. Both passed through the shopping areas of Acton, Harlesden, Willesden and Cricklewood where they parted company; good patronage came from factories in North Acton and railway workers at Old Oak Common and Willesden Junction, not only for these routes but also for the peak hour 626. Hendon was one of a number of depots to work the 666 over the years; it was renamed Colindale in July 1950.

For those travelling between Hammersmith and Acton Market, it was quicker to use a 660/666 rather than a 626/655; only joyriders would use the latter services between these places. It was also ten minutes quicker to use a 628 between Hammersmith and Craven Park as opposed to a 660/666.

Trolleybuses are renowned for their rapid acceleration from start. Acton Technical School was situated at School Road North Acton; outside the Carltona Custard Powder Factory was the northbound bus stop for routes 626, 660 and 666. The last lesson on Friday afternoons was double maths and, from the blackboard, one of the form-masters had a clear view through the window on the top floor to see trolleybuses coming round the corner at North Acton Underground Station and advance towards the school. There always seemed to be one at 3.55pm. On seeing it, the teacher would allow the class to finish, knowing that the few quickest pupils were already packed up and would race down the flights of stairs, cross the playground, dash across School Road and flag it down before it went past. It was part of his weekly entertainment. On one occasion, a number of pupils managed to get to the stop but the only boy who made contact with the trolleybus soon found himself in trouble; he had been unable to board but was clinging to a platform handrail. He hadn't got the strength and agility to haul himself on board as the trolley accelerated away. The crew couldn't have noticed what had happened and he had no option but to run, dragged really, beside the platform all the way to the next stop, at the junction of Chandos Road and Victoria Road. The boys left on the corner of School Road were in hysterics as they watched his legs pumping up and down as he struggled to keep upright alongside the trolleybus. If he had let go, school uniform would have formed part of the roadway.

In 1958, London Transport decided to set aside trolleybus 260 as a representative example for their museum; it was the penultimate C class vehicle overhauled, being released on 17th January 1958. It was allocated to Stonebridge depot and a picture of it appeared on the front cover of the October 1958 issue of the London Transport Magazine with the title 'THE CHOSEN ONE'. Withdrawal was after service on 18th August 1959, stage three of the conversion programme; Clapham Museum must have been keen to take possession of such a prize exhibit as it was towed there on 27th August – a mere nine days after last operating in service. C2 260, on the 666, turns from Dalling Road into Glenthorne Road on 16th March 1959; in a few minutes' time it will reach Hammersmith. It is 8.35am and the proprietor of the Penguin Café should be open for business by now; with five pints of milk waiting on the doorstop, maybe he's overslept! This is a place where dewirements have occurred on a regular basis as 'fairy lights' are positioned between the two sets of running wires, and guard wires are strung between traction poles. (Peter Mitchell 12256)

Despite showing CRAVEN PARK (the conductor has prematurely changed the front blind for its next trip), 304 is on its way to Hammersmith on route 660. At the time this view was taken on a snowy 20th February 1955, trolleybuses curtailed here (by the Thatched House public house in Paddenswick Road) did so on battery and without a destination blind display. Towards the end of the year, wiring was erected so that trolleybuses can turn more speedily. (Peter Mitchell 6777)

This view shows the new set-up outside the 'Thatched House' in Paddenswick Road; trolley arms need to be swung from the main line to an un-frogged set of wires. These arrangements came into force in November 1955 and a PADDENSWICK ROAD display added to blinds manufactured after that. Not every Finchley trolleybus received a blind incorporating that display and conductors had to call out the curtailment point. On 16th March 1959, N1 1559, on the 666 passes the new arrangements where Paddenswick Road merges with Dalling Road. (Peter Mitchell 12257)

1613 worked at Bow depot from November 1939 until August 1959 when it was transferred to Stonebridge; it is 14th May 1960 and painted depot code plates have very recently replaced metal ones. This view was taken at Seven Stars Junction where routes 660/666 crossed the 657. The road layout did not lend itself to a 'straight' crossover so northbound 660s/666s have to use a short section of track adjacent to the 657 wires. A United Dairies shop is in view as is a Lyons van. (Peter Mitchell 14513)

Seen outside Acton main-line station on 8th April 1960, F1 660 works on peak hour route 626; its destination is ACTON (MARKET PLACE). 660 was one of a small number of F1s that retained their wire grilles until the end; now allocated to Hammersmith, it was the only trolleybus at the depot that had this feature in the run-up to the conversion. (Peter Mitchell 14269)

Almost brand new C3 334 is at Willesden Junction Station working on route 660 to Hammersmith. Both windscreens are open. Going the other way on the same service is C2 255 working to North Finchley. Advertisements are an effective means of business and are on hoardings and the side of a building. (Bus of Yesteryear)

At Harlesden Jubilee Clock, P1 1705 heads home to Hammersmith depot at the end of the evening peak hour one day in July 1960; the conductor pulls the frog handle down to allow 1705 to take the outer set of wires. After the last 626 from Acton passes through on 19th July – F1 656 on HB7 – the wiring which 1705 is about to use will not be used by trolleybuses in service again. The only time they might get a little bit of polish is if a learner vehicle passes through from Acton. (Don Lewis).

It is 24th August 1959, so 1617 has only been working from Stonebridge depot for six days (it had previously been at Bow). It is seen at Harlesden Jubilee Clock on its way to Hammersmith on route 666. There is a noticeable shine to 1617, an indication of staff keeping on top of matters. Stonebridge were reasonable with their cleaning but 1617 will lose its lustre in due course as it will be out on the streets for most of its remaining days. (London Transport Museum 23717)

D2 449 is in Station Road, West Croydon having left the 630 terminus just a couple of minutes ago. It is about an hour and a quarter run to Harlesden; the 630 was a busy service and many fares will be taken on this trip. (Colin Maggs Courtesy Colour-Rail)

The Grant Road terminus at Clapham could never be described as salubrious as shown by D3 499 which is enjoying a few minutes rest from its labours on route 628. The rear of a London trolleybus was as attractive as its front. Bowstring bracket arms were used in Grant Road. (P H Grace Courtesy Colour-Rail)

1401 on the 605 turns from Cambridge Road into London Road. This busy scene at Norbiton Church was taken in the run-up to the final stage of the London trolleybus conversion programme – a yellow 'Buses for Trolleybuses' poster on the traction standard on the right confirms this. (Fred Ivey)

COLOUR SECTION

The sands of time are running out for the London trolleybus as it is 8pm on Tuesday 8th May 1962. L3 1399 pulls out of Tolworth Red Lion loop while working on route 603 to Richmond Park. 1399 has performed two more journeys since the picture taken at the top of page 58. (John Clarke)

A busy scene in Hounslow High Street sees 1074 on its way to Shepherds Bush on route 657. There is a lot of vehicle and pedestrian movement; this contributes to the late running of trolleybuses. (Tony Belton)

753 was the highest numbered F1; vehicles in this class were an all Leyland products – both the chassis and body were of this marque. 753, at Boston Manor Station, heads for Hammersmith on route 655 on a sunny 21st July 1959. (John Clarke)

L3 1381 crosses the Grand Union Canal while working on route 667 to Hampton Court. 1381 is advertising Guinness beer and Typhoo tea; this vehicle was the first of 289 trolleybuses to carry an FXH registration. (Tony Belton)

COLOUR SECTION

K1 1114 is at the bottom end of Goldhawk Road while working yet another trip on route 657 to Hounslow. It is allocated to Isleworth depot who always turned out their vehicles in tip-top condition. A sign on a traction standard directs people to Stamford Brook Station. (Tony Belton)

A very smart looking 715 on route 607 is seen at Brent Bridge, Southall on 21st July 1959; it had been released from overhaul the previous October so the Hanwell cleaning staff have done a good job keeping her 'spick and span'. 'News of the World' adverts are prominently displayed on 715. The bridge in the background takes trains from Paddington to the West of England. (John Clarke)

COLOUR SECTION

Q1 1768 pulls out of Uxbridge but is only going as far as Hanwell Broadway on route 607. This vehicle was withdrawn on 8th November 1960 and placed in store; despite the Q1s' imminent withdrawal, it entered the overhaul system and was not released until February 1961. It was re-licensed to Isleworth on 1st March to work on route 657; during the day of 25th April it was moved to Fulwell for another spate of storage. (John Laker)

C3 327 passes the crossover at Paddington Green while working on route 662 on 10th April 1959, the conductor has already changed the front destination blind for the return trip to Sudbury. The front advertisements were colloquially known by some enthusiasts as 'The Backward Twins'. 327 was one of one hundred and two London trolleybuses fitted with rear wheel spats. (John Clarke)

It is Tuesday 19th July 1960, the last day that Hammersmith depot will be operational; they have put out F1 743 on route 630. The vehicle will not die with the route for she will be transferred to Hanwell depot that night; it was the intention that she would remain in service until stage eight of the conversion programme. However, she failed a few days beforehand and was withdrawn prematurely. (John Clarke)

L3 1521 is in Craven Park Road, Harlesden while working on route 660 to Hammersmith. This vehicle spent most of its time in the East End but the conversion programme saw it moving to Finchley depot; a further move would see it at Fulwell where in the small hours of 9th May it became the last London trolleybus to operate. (Denis Battams)

Colindale's 329 picks up a number of passengers in Chichele Road, Cricklewood. The 666 was always a busy service and the crew will have to work hard to keep to time. Note that the bus stop has been positioned beyond the overhead section breaker; this was good thinking as the driver can make a clean get-away. (P H Grace Courtesy Colour-Rail)

N1 1582 is at the Canons Park terminus of route 645 and working as CE 11 on what is obviously a hot summer day. Colindale depot only have a small number of vehicles to look after and have time to keep their vehicles in good condition – note the gleaming paintwork on the nearside. (John Laker)

C3 313 is allocated to Finchley depot and is in Kingsway, North Finchley on 10th April 1959; it is another vehicle with rear wheel spats. The conductor has altered the front blind for the next trip to Holborn Circus on route 521. There is no doubt that Radio Times are cranking up the ante. (John Clarke)

NORTH-WEST LONDON

PADDINGTON TO SUDBURY

Route 662 worked from Sudbury to Paddington, passing through Wembley, Harlesden, Kensal Green and Ladbroke Grove; the only place of note between Harlesden and Paddington was Kensal Green Cemetery! The 662 was not plagued by traffic problems and only in the run-up to Christmas were short-workings often seen – College Park and Wembley Hill Road. On the Saturdays when the Amateur Cup Final and the Association Football Cup Final were held at Wembley Stadium, trolleybuses were drafted in from other depots to cope with the demand; extras, which could park on the lengthy siding here,

were also provided when international games took place on weekday evenings. Most were crewed by Stonebridge staff. The Harrow Road was used by the 662 from one end of the route to the other; only the infrequent 18B and a Sunday 18 route gave 662 crews a respite from a continual stream of passengers. At College Park, a connection was made with trolleybus routes using Scrubs Lane. Although Paddington was known by London Transport as a Central London terminus this was not so, as it was a fair distance from anywhere that could be deemed Central London; in fact, trams got closer to the Edgware Road than the trolleybuses.

The overtaking wire at Paddington Green was a useful facility; it allows Colindale's 325 on the 664, to overtake Stonebridge's 276 on route 662. Due to more frequent winding, destination blinds needed to be replenished more regularly than route blinds. The Charlton produced linen route blinds on both trolleybuses have survived; their destination blinds are 'paper' produced items from Aldenham Works. (Alan Cross)

Route 662 operated at a two/three minute headway at peak times so it is not surprising that two are running together on the morning of 16th March 1959. C2 281 and C3 308 survived the mid-1950s service cuts and continued to operate from Stonebridge depot until August 1959 and November 1959 respectively; 281 has 'ordinary' mudguards while 308 has 'spats' fitted over them. Another difference between the two is that the route numbers and destination blinds are in different styles of print. This view was taken at Chippenham Road on the Harrow Road. (Peter Mitchell 12259)

To cope with the number of football fans requiring transport to Wembley, 1561 is an EXTRA to STADIUM WEMBLEY HILL ROAD; it has just turned out of Letchford Gardens into Harrow Road. Its trolley arms move from 630 wires to those of the 662. (Fred Ivey)

An animated scene at Jubilee Clock, on 24th June 1960, sees 1558 heading for STADIUM WEMBLEY HILL ROAD on route 662; it is immediately behind another 662 with a passenger prepared to alight at the next stop. Going the other way, is an RTL on route 18B. (Peter Mitchell 15307)

K2 1160 is just a few minutes into its journey from Craven Park to Clapham Junction on route 628 on 2nd July 1960; it has just passed Manor Park Road in Craven Park Road. Trolleybus conversion stage seven occurs in a little over a fortnight's time and 1160 will be passed from Hammersmith to Stamford Hill depot. However, the Stamford Hill foreman will reject it due to its poor condition and it will go for scrap; however, the Hammersmith maintenance staff had considered it to be in good repair. (Peter Mitchell 15341)

This view encapsulates a typical London trolleybus in action; allocated to Stonebridge depot 262 passes through Craven Park on its way to Paddington on route 662 on 3rd April 1959. C2 262 was formally withdrawn on 19th August 1959. Along with a number of other C class vehicles, it was driven by Stonebridge engineers to Colindale scrapyard the previous evening on the basis that it had been sold on 18th August – yet it was still in service that day! Could Cohen's have claimed a day's hire from London Transport? (John Clarke)

N1s 1557 and 1593 have both run into Stonebridge depot after working on route 660 one day in the summer of 1961. Those parking the two vehicles are professionals for their booms are just inches apart. The blinds on 1557 are well set – that cannot be said for those on 1593. (Don Lewis)

The snow of 31st December 1961 saw the remaining trolleybus services thrown into chaos and inspectors had to work hard to give some semblance of regularity to them. Seen at Marks Park on 2nd January 1962 (a quarter of a mile away from Stonebridge depot) 1668 and 1639 are not running the full length of the 662 to Paddington. Although 1668 is showing ACTON VALE HARLESDEN it has to be assumed that it is running to College Park – maybe the blind handle is frozen. 1639 is running into Stonebridge depot – the only way it's going to get in is for the poles to be pulled down and battery mode used. (Tony Wright)

Cup Final days saw many extras supplied by Stonebridge depot; having brought fans to the match as the fourth extra, a gleaming 298 shows EXTRA CRAVEN PARK STONEBRIDGE. The conductor has used his initiative as 298 has to travel to Craven Park to turn to get back to the depot; it just saves him an extra blind wind and does not dissuade passengers from boarding. (Fred Ivey)

2nd May 1959 was Cup Final Day and Luton Town played Nottingham Forest who won 2–1. To provide additional transport for fans, Stonebridge ran many EXTRAS which turned at STADIUM WEMBLEY HILL ROAD. It is 4.31pm and C3 354 leads two others round the loop; they will park on the siding there – others will join them in a few minutes time. Once the game is over, supporters from both teams will fill all trolleybuses heading east for quite a time. The extras provided good overtime for Stonebridge staff. (John Clarke)

Virtually one year later it was Cup Final Day again – Saturday 7th May 1960 and the classes of trolleybuses now at Stonebridge depot has completely changed. They have dispatched a number of extras to deal with crowds leaving Wembley Stadium – it is 4.42pm so London Transport have got themselves well organised as the match was due to finish at 4.40pm. Although 1556's destination blind shows HARLESDEN CRAVEN PARK it does not necessarily mean that it is only making that short trip – this display may have been left up when it last ran into Stonebridge depot. Its next journey will be to inspector's instructions; he is stationed at the loop on the other side of the road. Wolverhampton Wanderers beat Blackburn Rovers 3–0. (Peter Mitchell 14482)

The E1 class comprised fifty vehicles which were originally allocated to Ilford, Walthamstow and West Ham depots; the Ilford contingent departed in wartime. The mid-fifties service cuts saw all of Walthamstow's and some of West Ham's E1s move to Stonebridge; 555 is formally recorded as arriving from Walthamstow on 1st June 1955. It approaches Sudbury on 29th July 1959. E1 555 does not have many more days in front of her for with the imminent arrival of N1s from Bow she will be taken out of service on the night of 18th August. (Peter Mitchell 13470)

The photographer saved his pay during his stint in the army; putting money away each month meant that when he returned to 'Civvy Street' he had enough to purchase a top class camera at the cost of £190 – in today's money it would cost £5,210! Its quality meant that even the individual snowflakes are caught in this view of 1608 at Sudbury roundabout on the afternoon of Sunday 31st December 1961. The destination blind shows Paddington – this 662 has no chance of it getting there on time though. (Peter Mitchell 19699)

HARLESDEN TO CRICKLEWOOD

Route 664 operated between Paddington and Edgware, having commenced on 23rd August 1936; three weeks earlier, on 2nd August, the 645 was introduced working between North Finchley and Edgware. The 645/664/666 served notable firms along the Edgware Road: Smith's Clock Factory at Cricklewood: Staples Mattresses at Staples Corner: Duples Coachworks, Schweppes and Benskin's Brewery all at West Hendon. A big organisation, Frigidaire (opposite Colindale depot) had a large workforce who patronised the trolleybuses. These three routes, along with bus routes 60 and 142, 'spread the load' between Colindale and Cricklewood. The 645 was simultaneously extended to Canons Park and Barnet on 1st June 1938. An example of trolleybus operation, not possible on Central Buses, were three Monday to Friday morning peak hour trips from Paddington to Acton Market or Bromyard Avenue, Acton Vale (none the other way in the evening peak). The 645/660/664/666 group of services were the most profitable of the trunk trolleybus routes operated by London Transport. At trolleybus-dominated Harlesden, there were two major overhead junctions within half a mile of each other – Craven Park and Jubilee Clock; routes 628 660, 662, 664 and 666 worked this section with virtually a trolleybus in sight all the time. Trolleybuses could be held up through events out of their control and when the annual Sunday Willesden Carnival took place, delays ensued. Route 664 became a peak hour and weekend service in May 1956; it last operated on 6th January 1959. From the following day the 666 became a daily service but with passenger levels falling, the 662 was not boosted as

part replacement of the 664 – crews just had a harder time on the Paddington to Harlesden stretch.

Flexibility was the order of the day on trolleybuses and the covering of gaps on the 645 to Canons Park was met by one of two means. (1. A 645 would carry out two Canons Park/Cricklewood journeys instead of going to Barnet, or a 666 would perform two similar trips instead of going to Hammersmith; crews would comply as it was an easier option. (2. A 664 or 666 could be projected beyond Edgware; a one-lined CANONS PARK display was added to Stonebridge blinds for this. An unofficial movement occurred one Sunday morning when a Stonebridge driver decided to go up to Canons Park (Edgware was his terminus) to 'see what it was like'. First 645s did not start until 10am so he knew that he would avoid observation. He would have had to be a man of quick thinking if he had been asked to explain this movement, if for any reason he had been unable to return from Canons Park. For those travelling between Canons Park and Barnet it was significantly quicker and cheaper to use bus route 107 rather than the 645. However, there were those who would travel on a summer Sunday between its two termini as it was a nice run through suburbia with a rural atmosphere at its outer ends.

During the Suez Crisis (late 1956/early 1957), London Transport placed an embargo on the use of motorbuses for staff 'private hires'; this led to the unfortunate cancelling of a number of outings for staffs' children at the Christmas and New Year period. However, trolleybuses were not affected and a number of bus garages called upon their trolleybus counterparts to help them out. Bus and trolleybus staff were usually fierce rivals (particularly

In Church Road Harlesden at its junction with Conley Road, C231 heads for Paddington on the 664 at mid-day on March 13th 1955. Receiving a full overhaul six months later ensured that it stayed in service until 18th August 1959 by which time it was the second oldest trolleybus in the fleet – 208 held senior position. (Peter Mitchell 6821)

The snow of Sunday 31st December 1961 was so heavy that trolleybus services were still in disarray two days later – road conditions slowed all vehicular traffic. At 12.47pm on Tuesday 2nd January 1962, N1 1572 is on St Gabriels Church loop which is an off–line of route facility for route 645; it was running so late that it turned here rather than go to Barnet. It is CE3 on the 645 which was the running number of the last trolleybus scheduled to enter Colindale depot that night. However, vehicles were being changed over all day and sister vehicle 1564 carried out the last rites twelve hours later. (Peter Mitchell 19745)

Route 666 was stocked with C class trolleybuses from day one so this shot of 271 is more typical than views taken after 1959 when N1s/N2 s were used. 271 turns from Edgware Road into Chichele Road at Cricklewood on 3rd April 1959. Stonebridge's 271 will be withdrawn on the night of 18th August 1959 and will pass through Cricklewood when making its way to Colindale scrapyard the following day. Too soon to go really after a long time serving Londoners, but the stark reality of it all was that there was just no more work for her. (John Clarke)

C2 265 is by Mora Road on the approach to Cricklewood Broadway at the end of the morning peak on 28th March 1955; it has completed a tour of duty on route 666. Amazingly, the Charlton blind compilers have been able to fit STONEBRIDGE DEPOT onto one line on the destination blind. (Peter Mitchell 6903)

322's driver is one of Colindale's stalwarts and has driven trolleybuses for many years; therefore he knows the overhead wiring of routes 645 and 666 like the back of his hand. 322, working on route 666 to Edgware, is about to pass the entrance of Cricklewood bus garage on 18th July 1959; the railway bridge carries a freight line. Exactly one month later 322 will be withdrawn and replaced by a newer model from Bow depot. (Lyndon Rowe).

Just another mile or so to go and 590's faculties will not be used again. Withdrawn at West Ham at stage five of the conversion programme she went to Hanwell depot for short-term storage. E1 590 is at Staples Corner heading north to Colindale scrapyard in February 1960. (Fred Ivey)

Many of the major road arteries into London were used by trolleybuses – one was the Edgware Road which was served by routes 645, 664 and 666; Colindale, Finchley and Stonebridge depots provided vehicles for these routes. Stonebridge's 1623 is in West Hendon Broadway on the afternoon of 19th March 1961 heading for Hammersmith on route 666. (Peter Mitchell 16927)

This view was taken on 22nd February 1960 with L3 1476 having recently moved from Poplar to Finchley depot. It is working on route 645 to Canons Park and is at the junction of Kingsbury Road with Edgware Road at Hendon and opposite the derelict Benskin's Brewery. (Peter Mitchell 14095)

Route 645 was jointly operated by Colindale and Finchley depots; Colindale had C class vehicles allocated while Finchley had C3, J1 and J2 classes. As the Cs were equipped with low horse-powered motors, Finchley usually put out C3s so as to give uniformity to the route. With newer vehicles moving westwards in 1959, both depots operated higher horse-powered vehicles thereafter and various classes ran together indiscriminately. Finchley's 320 has just passed Colindale shopping parade on October 7th 1954 while working on route 645 to Barnet. The only time that people were likely to ride all the way from Canons Park to Barnet was if they were out for a Sunday 'jolly'. (Peter Mitchell 6455)

By the time that this view was taken towards the end of 1961 Colindale's allocation of vehicles had dropped dramatically. Not only were there the mid-1950s service cuts but the depot also suffered the loss of route 664 in January 1959. Standing on the forecourt is 1564 which has been on the 666, next to it is 1615 which is a 666 going to Edgware – the 645 route number has yet to be changed. Inspector Hatton ticks off vehicles on his time sheet. (Ron Wellings)

Come winter, come summer, the trolleys were going out and the snow of Sunday 31st December 1961 did not deter them. Parked next to Colindale's office block is 1583 which has been out for some time; 1569 has been on the road too. There is just enough room for 1569's poles to by-pass 1583. The conductor pulls the frog handle down to enable 1569 to turn left out of the depot. It is impossible to say which route each vehicle is on. (Hugh Taylor)

The 'arrival lounge' or 'reception area' for trolleybuses that made their own way to Colindale scrapyard was on the approach road to the former Metropolitan Electric Tramways Hendon Works. Wood Green's 1099 survived culling and withdrawal at stage ten of the conversion programme, it being the intention to keep it until stage twelve. A fault saw it withdrawn on 1st June 1961, being replaced by 1269 that day. 1099 was driven to Colindale depot being moved later to Cohen's. To all intents and purposes, 1099 looks in very good condition – the front and rear views on 30th June confirm this. The advertisers will have been informed that the contract on 1099 ceased upon its withdrawal. (Hugh Taylor)

Having served Londoners for twenty or so years, most trolleybuses ended up in Colindale scrapyard. H1 773 had worked at Wood Green depot for most of its life; withdrawn at stage six of the conversion scheme it was reinstated two days later at Stamford Hill where it survived until stage nine. It languished in store for a few weeks before making its own way to the Colindale extermination chamber. Ignominiously a bulldozer has pushed it into the position seen; its nearside lifeguard was removed in Stamford Hill for re-use. (Christopher Mann).

From left to right are four former Hanwell vehicles. F1s 743, 733 671 and 702 are behind locked gates; this view was taken from the back of Colindale depot. The tram track in the foreground leads to the former M.E.T works which is being used by Cohen's for storage purposes. (Tony Belton)

Once they were in the scrapyard, trolleybuses tended to get knocked about and vandalised. This is illustrated in this early 1960 view of SA3 1758 – a far cry from 19th August 1959 when she had been the last trolleybus to enter Ilford depot. Vandals have smashed windows and Cohen's wagons have pushed her around. The front nearside tyre is unroadworthy; tyres were hired from contractors and had to be returned. Presumably slave tyres have been put on 1758 and its good ones are back with their owners. (David Stevens).

A large number of trolleybuses from Edmonton depot which had been working for their living on Tuesday 25th April 1961 were quickly moved to Cohen's in the immediate aftermath of conversion stage ten. London Transport wanted them off their hands as soon as possible; not only did this free up space in the storage depots where they were temporarily held, but it also meant that scrapping could keep up to speed. The only identifiable trolleybuses in this sad view are 1170 and 1177 which have been reasonably well parked; because they are near the scrapping area, they will perish earlier than some that have been in the yard for some time. (Tony Belton)

The arrival of the last few members of the first batch of Q1s in early 1949 allowed ten Fulwell C1s to be released to Stonebridge. One was 180 which moves down the incline from Burnt Oak towards Colindale on 17th March 1955; the nearest road junction is Greenway Gardens. 180 is running into Stonebridge depot after the morning peak; route 666 only operated in Monday to Friday peak hours at this time. 180 will not be in service much longer; due to service cuts in the first half of 1955 it was one of a large number of vehicles withdrawn at this time. (Peter Mitchell 6841)

March 17th 1955 finds C2 220 approaching the main southbound loading point at Burnt Oak Broadway; it is working on route 664 to Paddington. The conductor has aligned the route and destination blind very well; it will be another four years before the driver has the responsibility of changing the front destination blind and memorising the order of displays. (Peter Mitchell 6840)

Until August 1959, C class trolleybuses predominated on the Edgware Road services; C2 224 on the 664 to Paddington and C3 302 on route 645 to Canons Park are near Redhill Hospital, Edgware. Whoever slept in the front bedrooms of the houses on the right would be lulled to sleep by the swish of trolley arms – what wouldn't any London trolleybus enthusiast have given to have one of those houses as their abode? 245 belongs to Stonebridge depot and 302 to Finchley; 245 uses linen blinds while 302 uses 'paper' ones. This view was taken on 13th March 1955. (Peter Mitchell 6831)

A surprise in March 1961 was the allocation of four L2s to Stonebridge depot (they had been withdrawn at Highgate depot at conversion stage nine and put in store). They replaced some Stonebridge vehicles that had fallen by the wayside; a re-activated 1377 stands at Edgware terminus. The bus stop flag has a 666 E plate in place. (Fred Ivey)

N1 1628 turns through the dual carriageway in Edgware High Street on 27th August 1961; this was always a tight turn and 1628 is on full lock; the front offside panel has had a bit of a bump. In a few minutes time 1628 will head for Hammersmith on route 666. (Peter Mitchell 18683)

Only four minutes running time was given for 645s to get from Canons Park to the main loading point at Edgware; drivers and conductors had to be quick off the mark to achieve this. N1 1578 is in Edgware High Street on 21st August 1960. It moved from Bow depot to Colindale on 18th August 1959 and is as much at home in north London as it was in the east. (Peter Mitchell 15772)

C3 367 circles Canons Park roundabout on 4th October 1958. It will shortly come to a halt on the 645 stand where the crew will have a few minutes break. The conductor will have no idea whatsoever that this is the last day that the ticket rack and bell Punch system of fare collection will be used by his employers, as it occurs in the East End – at Poplar and West Ham depots. (Peter Mitchell 12070.)

on the same length of roads), but seasonal goodwill prevailed and the following is an example. Laurie Akehurst had the good fortune of having a father who was a bus conductor at Cricklewood Garage and relates: 158 people (mostly children) associated with Cricklewood garage had been expecting to attend a circus at Harringay Arena on 5th January 1957; to avoid disappointing such a large number of youngsters, a few phone calls solved the problem. At the appointed time that afternoon, the children (and some Cricklewood garage staff) gathered outside Cricklewood garage. Three trolleybuses from Stonebridge depot, all showing PRIVATE, passed by heading for Colindale depot where each turned round and came back and parked on the north side of the Edgware Road; all had their trolley arms dropped and the children were escorted across the road and onto the vehicles. Once everyone was on board the trio departed. At Cricklewood Broadway the vehicles turned left to North Finchley where they had to battery past a number of parked vehicles in the bus station. They then followed the wires through East Finchley and onto Nags Head Holloway where they turned left into Seven Sisters Road for Manor House; here they turned left into Green Lanes with disembarkment outside the arena.

Having dispatched the happy children, the trolleybuses headed north and parked up in Wood Green depot. The crews had been given an estimated time of the performance finishing and ran down to Harringay where again the trolley booms were stowed. Once the children had all been accounted for, the three vehicles departed and followed the same line of route on their way back, save for changing trolley arms in Kingsway at North Finchley rather than traversing the bus station. Everybody got off outside Cricklewood garage and the three trolleybuses made their way to Colindale depot, where once again they turned and went back to Stonebridge. Each trolleybus ran 28 miles with a total cost to the staff of £2.3/6d. The crews from Stonebridge carried out this work on a voluntary basis; however, staff working on private hire jobs had to be paid one penny each by London Transport and this princely sum would have been put in their pay packets in due course. The Stonebridge drivers would have known their way to North Finchley but would have been at a loss beyond there. Maybe the leading driver was a man who stepped up as an instructor when need be – he would have known all the overhead junctions for the trip.

CRICKLEWOOD TO BARNET

Routes 645 and 660 headed north from Cricklewood. Soon after passing beneath main line railway bridges in Cricklewood Lane, an unofficial but frequently used battery turn was sited, slightly north, at Gillingham Road. Beyond Golders Green, another battery turn – this time official – was located at Holly Park. It had been a notional turning point since inception but traffic delays in later years saw it being used frequently. No destination blind display was provided until April 1960 when HOLLY PARK was added to Colindale, Finchley and Stonebridge blinds – this was the last new display created on London trolleybuses. Passing through Temple Fortune, these routes reached North Finchley where the 660 terminated. With the withdrawal, in February 1946, of peak hour journeys on route 2 beyond Golders Green, the trolleybuses were on their own between Golders Green and North Finchley; it was here that the 645 was joined by route 609 to head north and terminate outside Barnet Parish Church. The Middlesex/Hertfordshire county boundary had been passed at Lyonsdown Road so for the last mile and a half, the 609 and 645 operated in Hertfordshire; they were one of two sets of routes to do this. For a few months in 1938, route 651 operated from Cricklewood to Barnet – it was replaced by an extension of route 645. On a few bank holidays in the late 1930s, routes 517/617 were formally pushed through to Barnet. Routes 645, 660, 662 and 666 were conversion stage thirteen; three days beforehand, the heaviest snowfall for many years swept across London causing chaos to service provision for their last seventy-two hours. Despite this, crews turned out in force at Colindale, Finchley and Stonebridge depots on the night of 2nd January 1962 to welcome home their respective last trolleybus.

It is just after midday on 2nd January 1962 and trolleybus services in north-west London will come to their conclusion in about twelve hours' time. Road conditions are starting to improve after the snowfall of two days earlier. 1458 turns from the Edgware Road into Cricklewood Lane while working on route 645 to Barnet. (Peter Mitchell 19738)

The intense snow of Sunday 31st December 1961 had a dramatic effect on the remaining trolleybus services. Road conditions were so bad that curtailments were the order of the day on 1st January 1962; Stonebridge's 1602, working on route 660, uses the battery turn at Gillingham Road which was situated off Cricklewood Lane, north of the Broadway. The manoeuvre was not without incident. First of all, the bamboo pole slid off the icy positive trolley boom when the conductor attempted to stow it; the trolley arm waves in the air. The conductor then pulled both poles down so that 1602 could reverse into Gillingham Road. The sequel to this was the conductor attempted to put one pole back on the wire at the same time as his driver decided to run 1602 down Cricklewood Lane on gravity. The last the photographer saw of all of this was the conductor sliding down Cricklewood Lane holding onto a trolley boom for dear life via a bamboo pole! (Hugh Taylor)

Having turned off Finchley Road into Cricklewood Lane, Colindale's 347 is running late and has been curtailed at Edgware. It is 6th May 1959 and before long 347 will be withdrawn from service; in fact on Tuesday 18th August 1959, it will run into Colindale depot, the blinds will be taken out, her poles dropped and she will be parked up in the depot. She will move the short distance from Colindale depot into Colindale scrapyard on 3rd September. (Peter Mitchell 12685)

C3 378 was damaged during the war while working from Walthamstow depot; upon repair it became an experimental pay as you board vehicle resulting in the odd styling to the platform area and the positioning of its 'police' plate to the back. Once the PAYB trials had finished it was passed from one depot to another; it spent a couple of months at Finchley at the back end of 1950. Between North Finchley and Golders Green the 660 was bolstered in Monday to Friday peak hours, providing a very frequent service to and from the Underground Station. The previous frame on the film shows 378 in Golders Green loop so it has worked one of these 'shorts'. It is now in Finchley Road on its way back to North Finchley; 378's conductor is efficient as the side blind shows the correct short-working display for this trip – many would leave up the 'through' display. (Dewi Williams)

Route 660 worked between Hammersmith and North Finchley; C2 259 has a good load on board as it passes through Temple Fortune at 8.32am on a sunny October 6th 1954. Rochester gas lamps are used by the local lighting department. (Peter Mitchell 6452)

C2 237 is in Regents Park Road opposite Arden Road on 18th April 1955; C2 237 is allocated to Stonebridge depot and is on the 660 to Hammersmith. The advertisements for Chef Sauce and Dulux paint demonstrate the wide spectrum of businesses that used London Transport vehicles to promote their wares. (Peter Mitchell 7098)

Just what London Transport wanted! – a power cut the Saturday before Christmas! This occurred in West Hendon and delayed trolleybuses on 23rd December 1961. Once the 'juice' was restored 645s and 666s had to be adjusted to get them back on their running times – 1569 was extensively delayed and curtailed at Holly Park. Driver Charlie Armitage has 1569 in battery mode to turn from Regents Park Road into Fitzalan Road; conductor Frank Sharville (with cigarette in mouth) deals with the trolley booms – a bamboo slung over the shoulder was a regular stance of Sharville's. (Peter Moore)

Cows and London trolleybuses could only be seen at two places: on the fringes of Epping Forest where they roamed freely and at Fitzalan Road Finchley where the Express Dairy farm had a herd. 1638 on route 660 reverses from Finchley Road into Fitzalan Road on its traction batteries on 14th July 1961. HOLLY PARK was added to Colindale, Finchley and Stonebridge blinds in 1960 as the curtailment point was being used regularly. (Peter Mitchell 18305)

It is 6.14pm on 21st August 1961 and N2 1660, which is at Finchley Central, heads back to Stonebridge depot at the end of its day's work. The route number, 660, corresponds with the numerals of its registration number – this feature could be seen on a number of London trolleybuses. (Peter Mitchell 18632)

L3 1515 is at Wentworth Park on Ballards Lane at 6.14pm on 29th June 1961. It is operating on one of the evening peak hour trips to Golders Green; these catered for the surge of passengers coming off the Underground at these times. (Peter Mitchell 18148)

Consecutively numbered L3s 1516 and 1517 have been given a thorough hose-down and internal clean by Finchley general hands. These 'deep cleans' were carried out on a rotational basis and ensured that the trolleybuses looked good out on the streets. Both vehicles are parked on the 'in road' in Finchley depot; they will need to move out on battery power to gain the exit wires. (Chris Orchard)

There was enough spare space in Finchley depot for withdrawn trolleybuses to be stored before sale to Cohen's the scrap merchants. Two former Highgate trolleybuses (964 and 1543B) have had their front lights removed for use on other vehicles. 964's trolley booms rest against the roof girders. 1483 and 1502 have no fears at the moment. (Tony Belton)

All crew reliefs for Finchley depot staff working on route 660 took place outside Woodberry Grove, which was the stop before North Finchley. As always, the trolleybus has been parked just beyond the overhead feeder; this meant that the next driver had an uninterrupted start. 1449 awaits a fresh crew on 26th November 1961. (Peter Mitchell 19563)

One month and five days later (31st December 1961) and a fresh crew approach L3 1450 at the 660 changeover point at the top of Ballards Lane, North Finchley. The conductor and driver have trudged through the snow from Finchley depot in Woodberry Grove. There was no heating in the saloons of trolleybuses and only a small heater in the drivers cab. Trolleybus staff were hardy individuals. (Terry Cooper)

During the resurfacing of North Finchley terminus in 1956, vehicles used the adjacent Nether Street where an immaculate looking 290 on the 660 has by-passed another vehicle whose poles are being put back on the wires by its conductor. To the left, a tower wagon is in attendance. (Don Thompson)

1450 passes through Whetstone on Tuesday 2nd January 1962; two days earlier there had been a very heavy snowfall across the Home Counties causing chaos to the remaining London trolleybus services. 1450 was one that was caught up in it all on the Sunday. Although there are still slushy conditions, matters are starting to get back to normal and 1450 is attempting the whole trip from Barnet to Canons Park on route 645. L3 1450 was one of five Finchley trolleybuses that passed to Fulwell depot at stage thirteen, giving them an extra four months service. (Peter Mitchell 19728)

1768 was the third Q1 to be delivered – on 12th February 1948. A short while later it was used for braking performance, hill climbing capabilities and power consumption tests. These were carried out in North London and used Barnet and Highgate Hills for the climbing part of the exercise. The first view shows 1768 returning from Barnet and is at Lyonsdown Road, the county boundary between Hertfordshire and Middlesex. The second view sees 1768 ascending Barnet Hill. At no other time was a Q1 trolleybus seen in this part of London. (Quadrant Picture Library)

Descending Barnet Hill on 29th October 1961 is N1 1615 which was due to be transferred from Bow to Stonebridge depot at stage three of the conversion scheme. However, Colindale's 244 failed in mid-June and Bow were asked to provide a replacement at very short notice. The foreman probably grabbed the nearest one available and got it rushed over to Colindale. (Peter Mitchell 19438)

During roadworks at Barnet in August 1956, it was necessary to construct a revised turning circle within the already tight one there. The tower of Barnet Parish Church dominates the scene as 964 leaves for Moorgate on route 609. (Don Thompson)

993 was an unfortunate victim of wartime, being damaged in West Ham works on 30th July 1944. It was allocated to Holloway depot at the time and after a new body was constructed by East Lancs, it returned to its original home as 993B. It had a spell at Finchley depot between January 1957 and October 1958 during which time it is seen entering North Finchley trolleybus station while working on the 609. She has only just been able to get into the station as a number of other trolleybuses block the way. 993B was one of two rebodied trolleybuses that were allocated to Finchley depot – the other one was 1587A. (John Boylett).

L1 1366 is in North Finchley trolleybus station; this photograph was probably taken on a Sunday when the 517 only went as far as Kings Cross. The L1s were ordered in case route 611 had to be projected to North Finchley via North Hill; therefore they were fitted with coasting and run-back brakes. The extension never took place and the L1s were used indiscriminately on all of Highgate depot's routes.

1514 has had 'trolley trouble' while working on the 521 on 26th August 1961. Somewhere along the route a telephone call was made to the Finchley maintenance staff who attend to it at North Finchley. The positive boom is bent and is being straightened; it is held to the retaining hook by a piece of rope. 'On the road 'repairs meant that trolleybuses were not delayed. At one time the photographer lived at 170 Nether Street, London, N12. The Gaumont Cinema formed the backdrop to North Finchley trolleybus station throughout the trolleybus era here. (Peter Mitchell 18664)

1054 differed from other J3s in that the front had a streamlined appearance; it has just left North Finchley and heads for Holborn Circus on route 617. Parked, poles down, in the High Road is 1587A which was allocated to Finchley depot between November 1958 and November 1959. This view appeared on the front cover of the London Transport Magazine of February 1959 in which there was a feature about the forthcoming trolleybus conversion programme. 1054 had an ungainly end – its driver misjudged the line of the roadway to be taken under the Prince of Wales Road railway bridge at Kentish Town West on 15th November 1960; she was immediately withdrawn. (London Transport Museum U17454).

Four main roads come together at North Finchley with each being served by trolleybus. The 645 and 660 approached via Ballards Lane with the 609 and 645 heading up the Great North Road. Approaching via High Road Finchley were the 517/609/617; arriving via Woodhouse Road were the 521/621 which connected North Finchley to Wood Green – no other service ran along this busy stretch and inspectors had to ensure, one way or another, that a regular service was maintained. From North Finchley, the 517/609/617 passed through East Finchley on their way south to Archway where they joined the 611 from Highgate Village.

1447 spent almost twenty years of its life in East London – it had just nine months' service at Highgate depot in North London in 1960/61. Coming down the slope to East Finchley Underground station on 17th July 1960, it works short to Kings Cross on the 517. (Peter Mitchell 15489)

The turning circle outside East Finchley Underground station enabled late running trolleybuses on routes 517/609/617 to get back on time. This brilliant time exposure in the 1960/1961 winter sees 1667 on route 517 waiting out its time there. (Fred Ivey)

On 30th March 1955, C3 331 has just passed under the bridge which carries Hornsey Lane over Archway Road. 331 will have operated on route 609 to Moorgate many times during its career. The bridge was colloquially known as 'Suicide Bridge' due to the number of people who used it to end their lives. (Peter Mitchell 6097)

J2 1013 left Highgate depot a few minutes ago and is at Upper Holloway Station in the immediate aftermath of the withdrawal of the 35 tram route. This is a 'depot journey' and when 1013 gets to the Nags Head at Holloway it will join the 627's line of route; passengers can travel on this trip. A couple of dollops of asphalt have been placed over indentations in the tram track which will be removed shortly. (Courtesy Simon Butler)

It's an easy day for the Highgate shunters as only three trolleybuses have arrived at the entrance; running-in after working on the 517, J3 1048 is the back-marker. On busy days, trolleybuses would bank up almost as far as Holloway Road. (Alan Cross)

1051 climbs Highgate Hill on its way to Highgate Village on route 611 on 21st April 1960; descending, 1049 works on the same service to Moorgate. Both J1a had been on loan to Carshalton depot for nine days in September 1958. (Peter Mitchell 14386)

As part of its testing, 1768 ascended and descended Highgate Hill. Only coasting and run-back braked trolleybuses were allowed on the hill so maybe this part of the excursion was carried out 'on the quiet' or maybe by 'a nod of the head' via a telephone call to the Ministry of Transport. 1768 returns from Highgate Village and is on the section of Highgate Hill that needed coasting brake equipment. (Quadrant Picture Library)

The first J3, 1030, has just left Highgate Village terminus for yet another mundane trip to Moorgate on route 611 on 17th August 1958. The driver should be putting the vehicle in coasting brake mode about now. (Peter Mitchell 11704)

Posh Highgate Village was served by trolleybus route 611. On 24th June 1960 L1 1367 moves onto the stand which is to the left but out of view. The run-back and coasting-braked vehicles used on the route should have been withdrawn when the 611 succumbed; however, a number of J3s and L1s were reprieved and lasted until conversion stage nine. (Peter Mitchell 15306)

This view on 12th July 1952 shows the vastness of Highgate depot; trams have been gone for just three months but their tracks remain. The depth of the depot is very apparent as is the troughing in the south-east bay – one set has a pronounced curve to it. It is a Saturday when most vehicles are on the road; also in view are some withdrawn B2 trolleybuses. (John Gillham)

There were two exits from the Pemberton Terrace end of Highgate depot; this view shows the northern one. Note the tower wagon shed and its occupant. It is Saturday 12th July 1962 exactly one week since London's last trams ran. (John Gillham)

Highgate operated routes 513/613/615/639 – line of route from the depot was: Pemberton Gardens, Junction Road and Fortess Road; this meant that Tufnell Park only saw trolleybuses on 'depot journeys'. Conductors were instructed to show a blank route number on this section; 1051's conductor has complied in this view of it heading towards the depot just north of Tufnell Park Road. The conductor of 1577 is not obeying instructions as 513 is displayed as it traverses the very short Fortess Walk. The blind display of JUNCTION ROAD MONNERY ROAD was shown when working back to Highgate depot. The photographer has done his homework on 22nd July 1959 and caught both 1051 and 1577 running in after the morning peak. (John Clarke)

The turning circle at Parliament Hill Fields was 'tight' to manoeuvre and drivers had to 'get it right'. It is 9th January 1961 and reasonably quiet; on busy summer days the place teemed with activity. 1390 is on route 613. (Tony Wright).

Revised turning arrangements came into force at Parliament Hill Fields in October 1960; this saw trolleybuses use a lay-by rather than wait in Hampstead Road. 1429 uses the new stand in January 1961, waiting to depart for Moorgate on route 615. The destination blind does not sit well in the blind box. Many vehicles at Highgate depot had reduced depth destination blind panels; they were supposed to have the blind box masked so that parts of the preceding and following displays were not shown; as can be see this has not happened to 1429. The two ladies on the right – why is it that women walk around in twos arm in arm? (Tony Wright)

At Hampstead Heath, trolleybuses moved from Fleet Road into Pond Street – they then used South End Road and stood in South End Green. K1 1320 is in Pond Street with its blind already turned for its next trip to Moorgate on route 639. It is 11th December 1960 and 1320 will be withdrawn at the end of the following month. (Peter Mitchell 16532)

1551 on route 513 turns from South End Road into South End Green on 11th December 1960; its condition precluded it from being transferred from Highgate to Finchley depot in April 1961. Eight of Highgate's M1s made the move, thus gaining an extra six months' service. (Peter Mitchell 16533)

1398 passes though Camden Town while working to Moorgate on route 639 on 7th January 1961. A number of road signs assist pedestrians and motorists; the Underground bulls-eye is positioned too high for pedestrians to notice really! (Jack Gready)

On 7th January 1961 the first L3 -1380 – passes the trailing frog of Mornington Crescent loop; it is working on route 639 to Hampstead Heath. The 'advertising boys' are well ahead of themselves as a new newspaper, the Sunday Telegraph, will be published on February 5th. A big campaign was undertaken and many trolleybuses displayed their adverts; by that date 1380 will be working at Fulwell depot. (Jack Gready)